Extraordinary Praise for *Stressed-out Girls* by Roni Cohen-Sandler

"Cohen-Sandler's timely and relevant research and practical suggestions truly takes the area of girls' psychology deeper in a way that will help critically examine cultural norms. Understanding the five groups of girls who are at risk for serious stress and adjustment difficulties will help teachers, counselors, parents, and girls themselves better balance modern pressure for adolescents. If you care about girls, read this book!"
> —Norrine L. Russell, Ph.D., Executive Director, The Ophelia Project of Tampa Bay

"Cohen-Sandler offers action plans for fostering resilience and decreasing the root causes of stress."
> —*The Washington Post*

"An eye-opening, up-to-the-minute resource for all adults who work with teen girls."
> —*Booklist*

"Compulsively readable, *Stressed-out Girls* abounds with fascinating cautionary tales of well-meaning but misguided parents whose hypervigilant reactions to their daughter's stress (often manifested by falling grades) results in a downward spiral of family conflict, escalating antisocial interactions, academic apathy or rebellion, plummeting self-confidence, and risk-taking behaviors. . . . [Cohen-Sandler] is especially helpful in using real life experiences and shifting point of view analysis on where we, as parents, unknowingly make wrong turns in attempting to work through these issues."
> —*Wisconsin State Journal*

"[Cohen-Sandler] explores the pressures today's girls face to excel at everything—not just academically, but also socially and in sports and extracurricular activities."
> —*Connecticut Post*

"[A] wise, well-researched chronicle."
> —*Publishers Weekly*

PENGUIN BOOKS

STRESSED-OUT GIRLS

Roni Cohen-Sandler, Ph.D., has written for many national publications, including *Girls' Life* and *Seventeen* magazines. Her numerous television and radio appearances include *The Oprah Winfrey Show*, *Good Morning America*, *Today*, *The Early Show*, *The Montel Williams Show*, *CBS News*, and NPR. A frequent speaker for schools and professional audiences, she lives in Weston, Connecticut.

STRESSED-OUT GIRLS

Helping Them Thrive
in the Age of Pressure

Roni Cohen-Sandler, Ph.D.

PENGUIN BOOKS

PENGUIN BOOKS

Published by the Penguin Group

Penguin Group (USA) Inc., 375 Hudson Street, New York, New York 10014, U.S.A.
Penguin Group (Canada), 90 Eglinton Avenue East, Suite 700, Toronto,
Ontario, Canada M4P 2Y3 (a division of Pearson Penguin Canada Inc.)
Penguin Books Ltd, 80 Strand, London WC2R 0RL, England
Penguin Ireland, 25 St Stephen's Green, Dublin 2, Ireland
(a division of Penguin Books Ltd)
Penguin Group (Australia), 250 Camberwell Road, Camberwell,
Victoria 3124, Australia (a division of Pearson Australia Group Pty Ltd)
Penguin Books India Pvt Ltd, 11 Community Centre,
Panchsheel Park, New Delhi – 110 017, India
Penguin Group (NZ), cnr Airborne and Rosedale Roads, Albany,
Auckland 1310, New Zealand (a division of Pearson New Zealand Ltd)
Penguin Books (South Africa) (Pty) Ltd, 24 Sturdee Avenue,
Rosebank, Johannesburg 2196, South Africa

Penguin Books Ltd, Registered Offices:
80 Strand, London WC2R 0RL, England

First published in the United States of America by Viking Penguin,
a member of Penguin Group (USA) Inc. 2005
Published in Penguin Books 2006

10 9 8 7 6 5 4 3 2 1

THE LIBRARY OF CONGRESS HAS CATALOGED
THE HARDCOVER EDITION AS FOLLOWS:
Cohen-Sandler, Roni.
     Stressed-out girls / Roni Cohen-Sandler.
        p. cm.
     ISBN 0-670-03438-X (hc.)
     ISBN 0 14 30.3776 5 (pbk.)
     1. Teenage girls—United States—Psychology.   2. Stress in adolescence—United States.
I. Title.
HQ798.C56443 2005
155.5'33—dc22   2005042217

Printed in the United States of America

To my children, Laura and Jason,
with much love

Acknowledgments

First, I would like to thank my extraordinary agent, Loretta Barrett, for the integrity, dedication, insight, and careful thought that she brings to every situation. I also appreciate her ever-helpful assistants, Nick Mullendore and Gabriel Davis. A deeply heartfelt thank-you goes to Janet Goldstein, who was enthusiastic about this project from its inception and provided her usual intelligent guidance and meticulous attention. I am enormously grateful for the support of the entire team at Viking Penguin, especially Lucia Watson, Pam Dorman, Clare Ferraro, and Rakia Clark.

Thousands of girls and boys in middle school and high school made this book possible by generously giving their time and sharing their experiences—responding to my questionnaire, participating in focus groups, and speaking with me individually. I learned so much from them, appreciate their thoughtfulness and candor, and hope that I have done justice to the feelings, perceptions, and views they expressed.

I am indebted to all the heads of schools, principals, vice principals, guidance counselors, and teachers who saw the importance of this issue, gave me access to their students, administered the surveys, and spent time sharing their perspectives. To protect the anonymity of their students I am not thanking them by name. I am also extremely grateful to the earliest readers of this manuscript: Dr. Lyn Sommer, mother, psychologist, and writer extraordinaire, whose brilliant and incisive comments I have come to depend on, and Dr. Mary Monroe Kolek, whose insights into the education world and the hearts and minds of teenage students were invaluable. Karen Bokram, founder and editor of *Girls' Life*, Maria Drauss and her staff at Girls, Inc., Brenda Friedler, Judy Stanton, and Sharon Gilchrest O'Neill have my sincere thanks as well. As always, I appreciate the support of my Wednesday-morning peer supervision group, along with many friends who have generously offered their expertise, enthusiasm, and title suggestions, especially Nancy Magida, Dan Magida, Susan Earle, Cindy Mayer, Vicki Schonfeld, Debbie Rath, Jeffrey Jacobs, Jodi Susser, Michelle Tenenbaum, Lisa Foster, and Susan Feigenbaum. Special thanks to Weston Public Library for the use of their comfortable, quiet, and telephone-free conference room—a writer's delight—and, especially, to Westport Public Library, where they even permit refreshments.

Above all, I am fortunate to have a loving and supportive family: Arleen Cohen, Larry Cohen, Rose Sandler, and Sam Sandler. My son Jason's technical expertise, including his knowledge of spreadsheets, creation of color graphs, and emergency reformatting of my hard drive, proved indispensable in keeping chaos and panic at bay. My daughter Laura spent countless hours painstakingly reading through the final manuscript, making perceptive suggestions and correcting a potentially embarrassing oversight. Most important, I give daily thanks for my husband Jeff, whose constancy and love are my strength—and whose gracious pitching in keeps our lives running smoothly.

Author's Note

The personal experiences described in this book are based on actual clinical work and interviews. In all cases, however, specific details and identifying information have been modified to protect the privacy of the individual.

Contents

PART ONE

THE AT-RISK GENERATION

CHAPTER 1

Rising Nervous Energy: The Toll of Hidden Stress

By the time they enter middle school, many girls are staggering under the pressure of more than just weighty backpacks. They also face jam-packed schedules, hours of homework, heightened expectations, demanding social lives, and far too little sleep. For this generation of girls, the process of maturing into successful young women has become too intensely charged.

A hundred years ago, the famous educator Charlotte Perkins Gilman wrote that "the progressive education of a child should be, as far as possible, unconscious. From his first eager interest in almost everything, up along the gradually narrowing lines of personal specialization, each child should be led with the least possible waste of time and nervous energy."

Yet as I speak with groups of parents around the country, attend school events in my own community, and collaborate with colleagues, I often see that families intent upon raising accomplished children are doing exactly the opposite—and as a result find themselves in perpetual states of nervous energy. At PTA meetings, athletic events, and even on grocery lines, I hear mothers and fathers worrying about their daughters' grades in school, status with friends, progress in extracurricular activities, and chances of getting into first-rate colleges. Driving much of these parents' preoc-cupations are understandable fears that (1) their girls may not be doing well enough, and (2) there is something else they should be doing to help them succeed.

Adolescent girls express these same concerns. It does not matter whether I am speaking with middle school or high school students, either from urban areas or privileged suburban neighborhoods, or whether I am meeting with teens in focus groups or consulting pri-vately with them in my office. Almost without exception they tell me that they feel stressed by pressures to excel.

Although most look forward to seeing their friends in school, and many enjoy a particular teacher or subject, teen girls univer-sally dread seemingly insurmountable piles of homework and never-ending tests. They worry about completing their assign-ments well enough to maintain their grades—and also finishing them fast enough to keep up with their friendships and hobbies, practice their musical instruments, play sports, participate in school clubs, and look good.

And yet, despite feeling "totally stressed out," "overwhelmed," and "completely exhausted," many girls today think even doing all this is not enough. They believe they should also be doing every-thing perfectly. Responding to one of many harmful messages of this culture, they equate being *successful* with being *extraordinary*. These teens think that besides acing every subject, they must also star in their school plays, shine in music, excel athletically, be pop-ular, and win awards. Like many parents, these teen girls consider weakness in any area unacceptable. But such goals are unrealistic, if not impossible, to achieve.

Emily, my friend's delightful, spunky twelve-year-old daugh-ter, puts it this way: "I feel like I have to have great grades, be in good shape, eat right, do lots of activities, and have a mil-lion friends. It's hard for me, but some people are just able to do all this." With this mind-set, many girls develop the mantra, "I just need to work harder," driving a relentless, unsatisfying, and ultimately self-defeating quest for perfection.

IT'S A GIRL THING

Although parents often describe their daughters' experiences in middle school and high school as worlds apart from those of their sons', the extent of gender differences is rarely recognized. Boys are not immune to stress, but teen girls are far more prone to taking on intense pressures to succeed academically and socially. Girls also perceive that despite what boys may or may not accomplish during adolescence, males usually get higher paying and more prestigious jobs later on. How they process this information affects their views of themselves as well as their possibilities for the future. In general, these four factors distinguish teen girls from their male classmates:

View of School. Adolescent girls have a whole different way of looking at school, where they spend the majority of their weekday time and confront many of the hurdles to their success. Boys are typically unemotional about school; they see these years as a means to an end or a goal that simply needs to be achieved. Because they tend to look at the big picture rather than at the details that often preoccupy girls, they are not as reactive to the goings-on—or as inclined to take disappointments or setbacks personally.

For teen girls, however, school is all about the process. What happens throughout each and every school day—academically, socially, and emotionally—becomes a yardstick of their success. Every moment really matters.

Even relatively minor issues that accumulate throughout seven-hour school days aggravate girls' pressure. For example, one middle schooler recounted this classic, bad-day scenario: "A bunch of little things happened that weren't all that important, but it got under my skin. A stupid thing like the cafeteria lady yelled at me for putting my tray back in the wrong place and then I was late to PE because I forgot where I put my bag. My Spanish teacher was in a bad mood, I got a horrible grade on my English paper . . ." On and on, teen girls recall—and often discuss, obsess, and agonize about—the litany of dissatisfactions and frustrations that might never appear on the radar screens of their y-chromosomed classmates.

Importance of Relationships. Peer group acceptance is crucial for most adolescents. But as described by Jean Baker Miller in *Women's Growth in Connection*, girls' self-worth develops primarily within the context of their relationships. Their sense of who they are is based in large part on how they impact other people. Teen girls feel most accomplished in school not only when they get good grades, but also when they are in sync with the people most important to them. Unless girls see their friendships and relationships with parents and teachers as strong and satisfying, they do not feel truly successful.

That is why teen girls keep a running mental inventory of the status of all their relationships. They review puzzling conversations, ponder compelling social exchanges, and imagine how others perceive their interactions. Continually noting, evaluating, and reassessing the quality of these relationships gives girls a moment-to-moment reading on how others view them. Yet these efforts, which require tremendous mental and emotional energy, can further exhaust girls.

Of course, social ups and downs are inevitable. But by listening to teen girls, I found that each up and each down during the course of every school day really counts. Each becomes a measure, however fleeting, of girls' self-worth.

For this reason, a teacher's offhand remark, a parent's irritation, or a friend's baffling expression are often more stressful for girls than adults would imagine. More than boys, girls feel like failures when they think they upset someone, can't help a friend, or let down an adult. Accordingly, these everyday events affect girls differently and far more powerfully than they do boys.

Lucinda, a high school sophomore, came to me for therapy when she became increasingly depressed and lonely after being rebuffed by one of her oldest and closest friends. In our sessions she speculated incessantly about what might have happened, what she possibly could have done to provoke her friend's rejection, and how she might go about regaining her friend's good opinion. Around that time I was also seeing a teenage boy who told a similar story about a good friend who suddenly began to ignore him. "So what did you do?" I asked Tim. He looked at me quizzically for a moment. "I changed my lunch table," he shrugged.

Ability to Read People. Far more than boys, girls are socialized to interpret body language and other subtle nonverbal behavior. However, their skill at detecting nuances in other people's attitudes and feelings also makes them more susceptible to infectious pressures for success. Girls quickly pick up on the apprehensions of others that swirl constantly around them—in class, on the ball field, at lunch, and, especially, at the dinner table. Abbie, a high school student, says, "We have parents and teachers who almost always want you to be great in school, and they want you to also be great in anything you do after school. I've been taking Tae-Kwon-Do since I'm four; my parents want me to be as great as my brother."

Like a match, parental nervous energy about achievement ignites and inflames girls' own worries about whether they have what it takes to succeed.

Desire to Please. Girls are generally more interested in pleasing adults. It is the rare teen girl who doesn't, on some level, want to conform to what she believes her parents, teachers, and peers expect of her. So great is her desire for praise that she is often willing to take on lofty or seemingly unattainable goals. Just before she graduated from elementary school, for example, Kaylee wrote in an e-mail: "My parents want me to be a computer. I feel so stressed, it's like I have to get an A on everything. When I think about my career, I want to be a doctor for babies. I want to go to Yahl [*sic*], but I think I'm too dumb."

As they mature, girls feel even more stressed when the expectations of their peers and adults conflict. It's hard to satisfy everyone. For example, this is what Martina, a hardworking and determined teen, told me about the pressures in her largely Hispanic, urban high school:

> *Pressure comes from everyone—parents, teachers, media, friends, boyfriends, coaches. Teachers may want you to focus more in their class and get better grades. The media shows you stick-thin models, violence, and sex. Parents want you to do well in everything, to be beautiful and healthy, athletic and smart. Friends demand your attention and pressure you to be just like them. Coaches push you hard, wanting you to work hard and lose weight. Your boyfriend may want you to grow your hair, dress more sexy, or dress less sexy.*

THE HIDDEN ANGST OF GIRLS

This kind of virulent nervous energy is rampant among today's teen girls. And yet, it is often hard to detect, even for the parents and educators who care most about them and their success. That is because teen girls are diligent about hiding their pain. They go to great lengths to deny or minimize their distress, leaving even attentive adults in the dark about their true feelings and experiences.

Even when there is irrefutable evidence that things are not going well, girls are pros at reassuring their parents ("I'm perfectly okay!") or adopting an air of indifference to their mothers and fathers' concerns ("My grade isn't so bad; you should see what the rest of the class got!"). When they find themselves in hot water with their schoolwork, even girls who are typically forthright and reliable often make excuses ("It wasn't my fault my teacher got mad!") or lie ("Don't worry, I caught up with my work!").

These are some of the reasons why teen girls bury their anguish:

Fear of Exposure. Self-consciousness, which peaks during the adolescent years, inhibits many girls from revealing their struggles. They are afraid of being even more scrutinized by adults who already monitor their ups and downs. Amy says, "My mother is constantly interrogating me about my friends. If I tell her anything bad that happened, it just makes it worse. Then she has to know everything!"

Need for Autonomy. Teens are working hard to establish age-appropriate separateness from their parents. Thus they avoid admitting to weaknesses that could result in dependency. "If I show my parents my poor grade on my math test," says Tracy, "they're going to take over my entire life. They'll keep asking me if I studied, and then my dad will insist on helping me every night and probably confuse me more."

Fear of Repercussions. Almost without exception, girls are afraid of what their parents will do if they find out they are overwhelmed or struggling. Belinda says, "They'll make me see a tutor and I won't have any time to myself. And if I did really bad, they might say I can't go online anymore or go out with my friends on weekends."

Reluctance to Raise Parental Anxiety. Girls are keenly aware of the challenges in their parents' lives, such as jobs, poor health, marital conflicts, divorce, and single parenthood. They also know that merely mentioning their struggles in some area or another can instantly provoke or inflame their parents' worries. Skilled at empathizing, teens often fear "making things even worse."

Avoidance of Flaws. In the midst of developing their own identities, girls' self-confidence is already shaky. Unable to recognize that they are still evolving, they often see their deficiencies as permanent flaws—a view that is sometimes shared by adults. As Virginia put it, "Parents and society want you to be perfect. If you have one or two bad days, they think you're just this really bad person."

Comparisons to the Ideal. Girls' most obvious and available adult role models, their mothers, are middle-aged women who often have come to terms with themselves and their accomplishments. What teens don't usually see are their mothers' false steps, early mistakes, and insecurities, which women themselves have either forgotten or take for granted. Idealizing their mothers can inhibit girls from revealing their own struggles.

Stress Is the Norm. As they look around them and see their classmates hectically running around and complaining of all they have to do, girls believe these experiences must be normal. If they think their situation is no different from anyone else's, they may feel less entitled to object or to ask for help when they need it.

With girls so determined to keep silent, it is tough for even the savviest of parents to find out what they are really going through. Getting teens to open up about anything is notoriously difficult; coaxing details about how well they are doing or how they are really feeling about their successes and failures can be next to impossible.

The fact that many parents feel isolated during their kids' teenage years makes learning about their daughters' lives even more frustrating. When they do get together with other parents, knowing that their teens zealously crave privacy makes mothers and fathers think twice before sharing anything personal. This makes it harder to get support. So while parents feel swept up in the flurry of escalating nervous energy around achievement, too often they remain unaware of the stress girls endure. Too often they are at a loss about how their own daughters are coping.

I have to admit that for a long while I, too, underestimated the prevalence and pervasiveness of girls' hidden pressure. I thought that the hype about achievement was exclusive to the Northeast, perhaps to the New York metropolitan area, and surely to the more affluent, high-powered communities surrounding my own. Also, I believed that the girls who were brought for counseling were unusually vulnerable to stress. But I came to realize I was wrong on all counts. The truth is, the pressure to excel is a national phenomenon, and its consequences are wreaking havoc on the lives of teenage girls everywhere.

An extraordinary number of teenage girls who never enter a mental health office are also feeling stressed, discouraged, and misunderstood in their efforts to be successful. Some are trying valiantly to keep up with superstar classmates or siblings. Others would like to compensate for the failures of troubled brothers and sisters or to justify the sacrifices of hardworking parents. A few are living out their mothers' or fathers' own unfulfilled dreams.

Reluctant to reveal their pain, these ordinary girls are silent about their disappointments, ashamed of their inevitable mistakes, and nervous about their futures. Although many are going about their daily lives feeling sad and demoralized, if not despondent, they may act out their pain in a variety of ways not easily recognized as signs of distress. Their parents may not have the slightest idea how unhappy they are—or why.

I discovered this somewhat by accident. In preparation for an article I was writing for *Girls' Life,* a national magazine popular among preteen and teenage girls, the magazine posted a Question of the Week on their Web site asking readers about any pressures they were feeling to do well in school. This topic struck a chord. In response, I received hundreds of poignant e-mails from nine- to fifteen-year-old girls from across the country.

For example, Colleen reported, "I came home crying today because there's no time for me. I'm not even sure if my parents understand what it's like. They never had such a tough time compared to us 2000 kids. I wouldn't be surprised if we start dropping dead from anxiety attacks and heart problems before we hit twenty." Similarly, Anna wrote, "I definitely think that I am overwhelmed by schoolwork and the pressure that is put on me to get good grades by my peers, parents, and teachers. Sometimes I cry myself to sleep at night just thinking about a test. I honestly dread school every day. Every single day."

As I read one compelling, disturbing e-mail after another, it hit me that these young readers—who were so eager to pour out their hearts in the anonymity of cyberspace—seemed equally determined to keep their distress under wraps at home. Perhaps it was poring through this three- or four-inch stack of responses all at once that was so powerful. Or maybe it was seeing such distress spelled out in print. Regardless, I read these e-mails first in shock, then in horrified fascination, and finally with heartache and the idea for this book mingling in my head.

THE ABCs OF STRESS

With nervous energy skyrocketing, the girls of this generation need the adults in their lives to do far more than in the past. Along with general understanding and support, they need voices of reason to counteract both the stress-inducing messages they get from this culture and the demoralizing, self-defeating beliefs some of them persist in telling themselves. But for this to happen, parents and teachers first must recognize the distress underlying teen girls' attitudes and behavior.

Many signs of stress are so common that they are accepted as the normal, even expected, cost of leading busy, productive lives. What teen, for example, hasn't procrastinated in doing her homework, overreacted to a situation with a friend, or frozen while taking a test? What girl hasn't lost her temper, been moody, excessively tired, or occasionally used aches or pains as an excuse to stay home from school? It is the rare daughter who hasn't taken out her troubles on a younger sibling or stayed up until all hours and then been late for school the next morning.

Every parent and teacher should be aware of these basic truths about the insidious, sometimes devastating, effects of stress on girls throughout the school years:

Young Girls Are Afflicted. The first thing adults need to know is this: Stress for success is no longer exclusive to ambitious high school seniors engaged in the nerve-racking college-application process. The epidemic in this culture has spread to ever-younger girls, infecting those on the cusp of puberty as well as older adolescents. Too often I hear the voices of girls who already feel very tired and defeated, though they have yet to graduate from the relatively protected confines of elementary school.

Alex, for example, came to see me because her parents were puzzled by her sudden reticence about school and meltdowns at home when faced with nightly assignments. A petite ten-year-old with blond curls and enormous, widely set, ice-blue eyes, her baby face looks somehow seemed incongruous with her anguish: "The second I get home from school I start my homework and I work nonstop until dinnertime. I get headaches so much and I feel sick.

And still, I have to go to middle school. And then I have to go to high school. And then I have to go to college."

Middle School Intensifies Stress. By the time girls enter the early teen years and middle school, developmental challenges exacerbate stress in every area. On the school front, girls are suddenly asked to follow mind-boggling rotating schedules, keep track of a slew of due dates, and deal with an array of teachers—each with their own preferences, idiosyncrasies, and expectations. This is the sort of juggling expected of corporate CEOs.

Adding to these new demands are the social challenges, which by middle school rival or surpass academic ones in both intensity and importance. In general, girls feel desperate to reconnect with friends they may now see less frequently during the school day. They need to reassure themselves of these old ties by helping each other with problems and analyzing the details of all their unsettling social interactions. Well before they get to high school, girls say they face daily dilemmas such as whether to get sleep or good grades, whether to work on math problems or friendship problems, and whether to study history or reflect on their own lives.

A generation ago, tweens who had yet to enter the halls of high school might have been playing Parcheesi, dressing up their Barbie dolls, and jumping rope. Today these young girls are obsessed with calculating their grade point averages, managing their time, and getting into good colleges.

Pressures Skyrocket During High School. When the stakes rise in high school, so does the level of stress—for girls as well as their families. That is because the road to success is increasingly lined with specific checkpoints against which achievement is measured—for example, whether or not teens are in honors or advanced placement (AP) classes; whether their SAT scores are high enough; whether they are chosen for selective teams, music ensembles, or honors; whether (and by whom) they are invited to proms; and so on. Any one of these criteria can seem like the definitive word on whether or not girls are successful—or will be in the future. Jan expressed the pressures of many girls in high school when she told me:

> *The worst thing about eleventh grade is the pressure to get into a good school. My parents are pushing me to study harder. Plus, you get pressured by all your friends to spend time with them, to go to their party or hang out. Have this boyfriend; you need one. Or you get stressed about homecoming. It's a big deal. Are you going? Who with? Do you have a dress? And with all this, I hope I get into a really good school and don't die from the stress of applying.*

THE TOLL IS REAL

Such issues may be common, even classic, during adolescence, but they are worse today, and suffering from stress should not be accepted as a given. In fact, these are the harmful effects on girls' physical health and mental well-being and, therefore, on their ultimate success:

Sleep Deprivation. Perhaps the most blatant consequence is the widespread lack of sleep among teens today. Though they require eight to ten hours of sleep per night, adolescents generally get far less. Not surprisingly, when girls in middle school and high school are asked about their worst school experiences, they typically speak of exhaustion:

- ✦ "The stress, sleep deprivation, and depression that almost defined junior year"

✦ "When the pressure comes on all in one week and I get very little sleep"

✦ "Every time I have to work until two a.m. or three in the morning and then sit through class the next day with a headache as time stops"

✦ "Getting no sleep because of work; draining myself emotionally, physically, and mentally; and doing worse in school because of constant lack of sleep"

Girls are losing sleep for two main reasons. One, many are intentionally cheating themselves of sleep in order to do everything they need to do. As Tina describes, "I'm staying up later and later to finish homework, or maybe I just want to read something for fun, go online, or relax, but I still have to wake up just as early in the morning and start the whole cycle again."

Two, girls are deprived of much-needed sleep because of insomnia; according to a 2004 *BusinessWeek* cover story on sleep disorders, 40 percent of teens have trouble falling asleep or staying asleep. As girls often tell me, "My mind's going a mile a minute," "I'm too tired to fall asleep," and "I have too much going on." Regardless of whether they deliberately pull all-nighters to study or they toss and turn for hours in their beds, the fallout of sleep deprivation is the same.

Susceptibility to Stress and Illness. Lack of sleep and the impairment in thinking ability that results deprive teen girls of much-needed skills to ward off the effects of stress. In addition, because of their compromised immune systems, they are more prone to illness. Getting sick and being absent from school cause additional stress because teens miss key class work or tests, fall behind their classmates, and have to work harder to catch up.

Increased Craving for Stimulants. Exhaustion also affects blood chemistry, provoking unhealthy cravings for caffeine, chocolate, sugar, and junk food. (Many teen girls would be horrified to learn that chronic sleepiness is associated with weight gain, which causes more stress.) In one school I visited, a student-conducted survey had found that the majority of girls drank up to three caffeinated beverages daily for extra energy.

Insufficient Exercise. Surveys also confirm a harmful decrease in physical activity among American females. A study conducted by the University of Michigan, for example, found that nine- to twelve-year-old children are spending 60 percent less time playing outdoors. Tracking girls over a period of ten years starting at age nine or ten, the National Heart, Lung, and Blood Institute reported an 83 percent decrease in median activity levels. Thus, by the time they are older teens, many engage in no regular exercise other than gym class.

Poorer Coping Abilities. With a distinct lack of downtime, girls are less able to relax, sleep, read for pleasure, and exercise. This undermines their ability to combat both anxiety and depression. Similarly, without the benefit of solitary activities such as writing in journals, reading, and creating music or art, girls can't soothe themselves as well. Teens today are caught in a classic catch-22 bind: Too stressed out to take good care of themselves, they are that much less capable of dealing with tremendous stress.

Diminished Brainpower. Chronic stress also more directly threatens girls' success by eroding their brainpower. Without the restorative and memory-building benefits of a restful night's sleep, girls can't concentrate or think as well, and they learn more slowly. In fact, research shows that staying up throughout the night results in the same level of mental acuity as being intoxicated above the legal limit for driving in most states. It is no wonder that sleep-deprived people perform many kinds of tasks poorly.

Also, emotions powerfully affect cognition. This relationship is the focus of much scientific attention today. New methods of mapping brain activity are enabling neuroscientists to understand how feelings and cognition interact in the brain. For example, one group of researchers discovered that mild emotional states such as amusement and anxiety affect college students' short-term memory. Neither emotional state nor the task alone made a difference; what mattered was the mood subjects were in while they did specific tests.

Plummeting Self-esteem. Chronic stress breeds feelings of inadequacy as well. Girls who find they can't think clearly or perform well understandably lose confidence. Comparing themselves to the idealized role models that surround them in this culture, in their schools, and even in their own families, many teens fear they will never measure up. They stop believing in themselves. They lose heart, not to mention motivation. Eventually, they stop trying.

Researchers confirm that less successful students self-handicap. That is, they sabotage their performance by procrastinating, studying for shorter periods of time, and barely reading their textbooks. This posture enables them to excuse their anticipated lack of excellence. If teens don't give their all and do poorly, they can blame lack of effort instead of lack of competence. Girls would rather be seen as lazy than stupid.

This story is typical. A high school principal was asked to see a tenth-grade girl whose teacher had sent her out of class because of how she responded to a question. When the teacher asked her why she had gotten a D on a test, the girl had replied, "I wouldn't waste my time studying this crap." When the principal later spoke to her about this experience, she confessed, "I'd rather be bad than dumb."

Thwarted Success. There is one symptom of stress that few parents or teachers can overlook: declining grades. This makes sense. The sheer number of hours girls spend in school, with all its simultaneous and complex social, emotional, and intellectual challenges, makes it likely that problems will show up there first. It is hard for parents and teachers to dismiss, rationalize, or justify poor report cards or test scores. They are most often seen—and correctly so—as red flags for trouble, perhaps even as girls' unconscious requests for adults to sit up and take notice.

Less often, girls manage to hold it together, silently and cheerfully going about the business of meeting other people's expectations. These teens don't complain. In fact, they seem to do everything and to do it all easily. They are model students and perfect daughters, likely to elicit praise and gratitude from adults. In fact, they are often held up as examples for other girls to emulate. That is, until they reach a breaking point.

NO GIRL IS IMMUNE

It is worth stating the obvious: Not a single girl gets through school unscathed. No teen is immune to experiencing problems. The crucial question for educators and parents, then, is to what degree girls are adversely affected or even incapacitated by stress. Given how well they hide their pain, how can we assume that when they seem to be doing okay they are *really* doing okay? How can we know when teens' unhappiness with their activities, friends, or teachers; their struggle in a particular subject; or anxiety about their future is normal—and when we should be concerned? Which teens are at risk for full-blown crises?

Psychologists conducting research in the field of psychoneuroimmunology (PNI) may have some answers. According to a newly developed biopsychosocial model of health and well-being, unhealthy reactions to stress occur when life's demands overtax coping skills. Whether stress results in a lowered immune response, susceptibility to infection, or depression depends on mitigating factors such as mental outlook, optimism, and social support. Perhaps most interesting, the body's physiological responses to stress depend more on *perceptions* of inner resources than on actual coping ability. It is whether girls *think* they can manage—that is, self-confidence—that matters most.

This finding is consistent with clinical experience. Teens go into crisis when they believe their pressures are insurmountable. Whatever coping skills they have counted on in the past no longer seem to work for them. Some endure a traumatic event (for example, a parental separation or death), others a relatively minor incident (for example, a fight with a friend or a romantic breakup). But something tips the scales, or a bunch of little somethings converge at once: recovering from the flu, coming back to school after an extended absence, missing a social event, getting a bad grade, or ticking off a teacher. At some point, however, the teen in crisis reaches a critical threshold of what she can tolerate, exhausts her inner resources, and hits a wall.

As a psychologist who has been evaluating and treating adolescents since 1977, I know this for sure: More and more, my colleagues and I are seeing this kind of fallout from a myriad of stressors. A psychologist friend who has been on staff for seventeen years at a large, regional high school recently told me, "By November of this year, we had more crises than during the entire school year last year." She is not alone. Guidance counselors from across the country are reporting a sharp increase in psychological crises among students and, as a result, an overwhelming use of school resources.

National statistics confirm these anecdotal data. Serious mental health problems are not only increasing, but also occurring earlier in childhood. Psychologist Jean Twenge, of Case Western Reserve University, found that normal children ages nine to seventeen are presenting more symptoms of anxiety today than those treated for psychiatric disorders fifty years ago. A study conducted at Yale New Haven Children's Hospital found that within a four-year period in the mid-1990s, pediatric psychiatric emergency room visits rose 59 percent. Obsessive-compulsive disorders among youth are also skyrocketing.

Many stressed-out girls are turning to risk-taking behaviors such as using substances and engaging in inappropriate sexual activity. As one school administrator told me, "Girls who have to do well in school are very dutiful on the surface. They're not going to violate the dress code, for example. But their interior lives are much more buried. They get into a lot of dreadful things. Girls can give you all the information about drugs and alcohol and sexual behaviors. But as soon as they get away from schools and parents, they just unload. Weekends are pretty wild around here."

Although these teens are often thought of as troubled or rebellious, their behavior is actually best understood as attempts at self-medicating for anxiety and despair. This may explain a disturbing trend: For the first time ever, underage girls are using mind-numbing substances such as alcohol and tobacco at the same rate as boys.

Equally worrisome, these vulnerabilities to stress do not end with high school graduation. Ironically, with all the machinations of trying to get girls accepted into college, they are not doing as well once they get there.

The Higher Educational Research Institute at UCLA, for example, found that the emotional well-being of freshmen hit an all-time low at the beginning of the 2001–2002 academic year, even before September 11, 2001. As an article on student wellness in the American Psychological Association's *Monitor on Psychology* described, "At campuses all across the country, more undergraduate and graduate students are reporting depression, substance use, eating disorders, learning disabilities, and, most common, problems adapting to college life." Indeed, a 2004 study of 47,200 college students conducted by the American College Health Association found that 45 percent reported feeling so depressed during the past school year that it was difficult for them to function.

In response, a new federal law was enacted in October 2004 to provide grants to universities across the country to enhance mental health services on campuses. In addition to traditional therapies, colleges have begun to offer stressed-out students a variety of services—from massages to dog cuddling to biofeedback to stress-free zones.

But we have to do our part as well. To send off teens to college well prepared, we have to encourage them to develop healthier attitudes about achievement and better strategies for coping with stress. Once again, girls need more help in these areas. The same UCLA study found that freshman coeds rated their sense of health and well-being lower than that of boys—and were twice as likely to report feeling frequently overwhelmed by everything they had to do.

By hiding their suffering, however, girls deprive themselves of potential understanding, reassurance, and support from adults. If they are not aware of their teen daughters' inner lives and true experiences, how can even the most loving mothers and fathers know how to help them? Similarly, if teachers have no idea what is causing a girl to disinvest from school or sabotage her own success, how can they best intervene?

WHAT'S REALLY HAPPENING

To find out what is really happening with today's teens—why they are so stressed, who is most at risk, and who is most resilient—I surveyed 2,298 girls (691 in grades six through eight and 1,607 in grades nine through twelve) about their attitudes, pressures, and experiences with success. These students attended a variety of schools: public and private, coed and all-girls, religious and secular, traditional and alternative. By posting this survey on the *Girls' Life* Web site, I also heard from girls across the country. A comparison group of 625 boys (98 in grades six through eight and 527 in grades nine through twelve) also completed my questionnaire.

In addition to interviewing parents, teachers, and school administrators, I spoke with about a hundred girls attending middle schools and high schools—either individually or in groups, on one occasion or over the course of a six-week period. I interviewed many girls who were Caucasian, as well as a number of first-generation Americans whose parents had emigrated from South America, Africa, Asia, India, the Middle East, Puerto Rico, and the Dominican Republic. I spoke with girls from poor, working-class, middle-class, and affluent backgrounds; their parents' highest level of education ranged from less than four years of high school to graduate school.

What I discovered is that all girls, even highly functioning ones, can be toppled into crises by a constellation of circumstances: temperament, personality style, past history, school dynamics, and community cultures. Furthermore, these at-risk girls form five distinct groups, each sharing specific vulnerabilities and preoccupations. Of course, teens often exhibit characteristics of more than one profile and have different sensitivities to stress over time. But these typologies of stressed-out girls offer parents and teachers a framework within which to identify and understand teens' most common struggles, anticipate crises, and step in most effectively to avert them.

Girls who are perfectionistic, for example, are pressured by the consuming need to be exceptional. Because they fear making mistakes that could cost them their dreams or expose them as frauds, they avoid the risks that are often necessary for true discovery and accomplishment. Unless they feel sure of succeeding, they steer clear of challenges and stick instead to what seems safe or conventional. With this mind-set, even mundane events such as getting disappointing grades, annoying their teachers, losing games, or fighting with their friends can seem cataclysmic.

Teens who experience personal or family problems make up another group of vulnerable girls whose pressing concerns prevent them from being able to invest fully in many areas of their lives. Strong emotions such as anger, anxiety, and despair—which they typically have trouble managing—sap their energy and prevent these girls from thinking sharply, flexibly, and creatively.

Teens in transition also need to adapt to a suddenly changed world. That is why girls who are starting middle school or high school or transferring to new schools are particularly vulnerable to the effects of stress—as are their families. Nervousness about the unknown, as well as the need to acclimate to different surroundings and demands, challenges everyone's coping skills.

Another at-risk group is made up of insecure girls who long for peer acceptance. Their intense alertness to their classmates' judgments siphons off crucial energy better directed toward creativity and achievement. Instead of thinking about lessons and ideas, they obsess about whether their outfits are acceptable, what someone's behavior means, or if the comment they just blurted is really dumb. Insecure girls play it safe by fading into the background. They are loath to participate or speak up in class. In fact, they will do anything to avoid sparking debate, controversy, or possible derision.

Last, there are girls who feel undervalued at home or in school. Like square pegs in round holes, they don't fit in. Sometimes their interests are unlike those of their classmates. Or they learn differently. When their talents don't resemble those of their family's, girls feel different (read "inferior"). In addition to the typical stress for success, then, square pegs feel additional pressures to live up to the standards they perceive in their family or school cultures. If they're not round pegs, they feel like failures.

What I also learned from my research is that all stressed-out girls, no matter their specific issues, are prone to becoming estranged from their inner lives. What I mean is that even teens who are driven to achieve are so busy living up to others' expectations that they either don't develop or eventually relinquish their own goals. They are so focused on achieving external emblems of success that they don't get the chance to figure out what really excites them and gives them pleasure. They barely know who they are or who they want to become. More troubling, when accomplishments lose meaning, teens begin to feel bored and empty, states that I believe are related to the prevalence of serious problems such as depression, self-cutting, and eating disorders among young women today.

In contrast, I found that girls who have been given the chance to get to know themselves and to pursue their true interests are two steps ahead of the game. Teens who believe their parents and teachers have hopes for them that are realistic—and in line with their actual talents and passions—feel most equipped to succeed.

Equally important, I discovered that while affluence and having exceptionally accomplished parents can increase teens' pressures and obligations, other factors protect them. What really matters is how resilient girls are to stress; this is determined by their self-confidence, social acceptance, perceptions of being valued, and coping skills.

This is why intellect and fine schooling do not guarantee success. In fact, the research is clear: Most successful people are not necessarily brilliant, but they are self-directed and passionate about what they do. A twenty-year longitudinal study of learning-disabled individuals by the Frostig Center in Pasadena, California, corroborates the importance of resiliency. Researchers identified six attributes associated with long-term life success: self-awareness, proactivity, perseverance, goal-setting, effective support systems, and emotional coping strategies.

What this means is that all the ambition in the world is not going to make up for a poor work ethic, lack of integrity, disorganization, or trouble getting along with others. Graduating from an elite college is not going to matter in the long run if a teen feels stressed out, insecure, discouraged, defective, or resentful. Unless girls have their emotional and social houses in order, they can't focus their energy and fully use their talents. Being smart is never enough.

RAISING RESILIENT GIRLS

Although none of us can eliminate nervous energy, there is plenty we can do to help teen girls become stronger and more resilient. Demographics suggest there is no time to waste. With schools across the country scrambling to accommodate rising numbers of school-age children, the already intense competition for private schools, internships, scholarships, jobs, and, of course, colleges, is likely to increase.

As a psychologist, I work with many families interested in learning how to capitalize on their daughters' strengths, compensate for any weaknesses, and encourage the fullest expression of their talents. In my previous books—*"I'm Not Mad, I Just Hate You!"* and *"Trust Me, Mom—Everyone Else Is Going!"*—I guide parents to use empathy, respect, and mutual trust to develop close, empowering relationships with teen daughters. I also consult with educators, teachers, and administrators on the needs of individual students as well as the developmental issues and challenges of girls in middle school and high school.

Fortunately, I have learned that parents and educators can have tremendous influence, more than would be imagined, but only with the right perspective and sensitivity. This book therefore begins by describing the context of teen girls' stress, including the underlying cultural pressures and family dynamics that often contribute.

As the mother of two seniors, one in high school and one in college, I understand parents' desires to see children succeed. I empathize with the worries, large and small. Especially as our girls progress through school and the educational stakes rise, we want to see that everything is going well so they keep the doors to their futures wide open. If earlier problems linger, we may fear that their bad habits have become entrenched or that their flaws will never improve. And we imagine that once our kids go to college, it will be too late to help them.

Also, I am all too aware of how our own past triumphs, disappointments, and failures can provoke strong convictions about what our daughters *ought* to be doing. We all want our girls to have every possible opportunity, especially those that were denied to us. We all want our girls to avoid the same mistakes we made. But it is crucial to differentiate our children's interests and needs from our own and to keep a cool head in this atmosphere of escalating nervous energy. That is the only way to avoid blurring the boundaries and trying to live vicariously through our daughters.

The profiles in Part Two offer a framework with which to interpret what girls' behavior probably means. Learning about other teens, you can better assess when your own daughter or student's struggles are short-term, temporary developmental blips, and when girls could be spiraling into crises. This information will give you insight into what sorts of interventions typically work—and don't work—within in each at-risk group. For example, when does a perfectionistic girl who chronically procrastinates need a nudge and when does she need space or time? How can parents effectively help a struggling, brand-new middle school or high school student to adjust?

Whether you are supporting your daughter through a brief social rough patch, helping her overcome a sudden academic hurdle, or dealing with a full-blown crisis, Part Three gives you the practical tools. When is it wise to ask the school for help, and what is the best way to do so? What is reasonable to expect from teachers? If the school can't provide the kind of expert help your daughter needs, what is your next step? And when is a mental health or educational consultation advisable?

Like so many parents, you, too, may be finding that even your best efforts aren't helpful. To get a derailed daughter back on track, perhaps you resort to lecturing, cajoling, bribing, threatening, or punishing. Before long, stress permeates the household, provoking daily conflicts around what she ought to be doing—for example, whether her homework is done soon enough or well enough, whether she has the right friends, and how long she can use the Internet or the phone.

In the process, however, girls often feel increasingly defensive, misunderstood, ashamed, and angry. That is because no matter how delicately we may raise concerns, they hear one of two unspoken accusations: either that they are not trying their best, or that their best isn't good enough. Teens feel criticized, judged, or pushed to be someone they're not. In a flash, it seems, girls view us as adversaries rather than allies.

This book offers a fresh perspective. An inside look into teen girls' hidden stress will give you vital information that will help you to keep your own anxiety under control. The insights you gain about your own daughter will enable you to bolster her resiliency. As you learn what your next step should be, you will take it with confidence. Above all, you will be better equipped to stay close to your teen and maintain the sort of relationship that fosters her success.

CHAPTER 2

Walking Tightropes:
Cultural Pressures

A whole host of cultural changes is fueling the hype about achievement—and driving girls' relentless pressure to excel in every area of their lives. As Christa, a high school student, describes, "I think girls always feel like they're not good enough for society. That they're not pretty enough, popular enough, skinny enough, or smart enough. No wonder so many teen girls have problems like eating disorders."

The road to success has become as narrow as a tightrope—and as treacherous to navigate—with no room for the occasional misstep or stumble. As Christa says, "Girls are being pressured into being sporty, smart, pretty, and popular. Why can't we just be a little good at all these things? Why do we have to be great at everything?"

This is a good question. Among other things, girls are responding to increasing cultural pressures for academic success and accountability as well as a greater emphasis on precocious and specialized accomplishments. They are also facing more diverse, confusing choices in their social lives. These societal changes are affecting how school personnel deal with students and their families, the attitudes parents develop about achievement, and, in turn, how they guide and react to their kids.

With all these pressures, even the most resilient girls are hard pressed to get through adolescence feeling good about themselves and their accomplishments. To appreciate how easily girls can be toppled off the tightrope to success, this chapter will highlight what it could feel like to walk in your teen daughter's shoes.

A STRESS-INDUCING CLIMATE

The Achievement Frenzy

A multitude of significant shifts in education reform, the economy, and the workforce are intensifying this society's emphasis on measuring achievement. The most salient example is President George W. Bush's No Child Left Behind Act of 2001. Enacted to achieve equity in education for disadvantaged and minority students, this bill requires every state to set standards for proficiency in language arts, mathematics, and by 2007, in science as well.

No Child Left Behind set into motion a tidal wave of anxiety over standardized test scores that is cascading down from administrators and teachers to parents and kids. Because schools are now held accountable for students who fail to improve or to reach proficiency, kids' test performance affects their school's reputation and curriculum, the district's federal funding, and most recently, even the salaries of some administrators and teachers. The *New York Times* reported that Denver was the first major city to offer teachers financial rewards for their students' progress. With the stakes of standardized tests now so high, it is no wonder that there is a veritable frenzy among educators, mothers, fathers, and students.

Even young girls pick up on their parents' anxiety about how well they do. They fear messing up, forgetting what they know, or being embarrassed by their scores. Girls especially dread letting their teachers and parents down. In New York City, ten thousand third graders who failed tests for promotion were held back in 2004, twice as many as in the previous year. As they mature, girls become that much more aware of the consequences of their performance. Our teens know that an awful lot is riding on the tests they take. Some educators I spoke with predict a national crisis in the making. They cite this skyrocketing stress; the redirection of funding from the arts, physical education, and social studies; and rising dropout rates, especially in urban areas.

A Scarier World

The current climate of political and financial uncertainty is only intensifying our parental trepidation. On a daily basis newspapers are filled with reports of terrorism, the sagging economy, escalating unemployment, decade-long anxiety about job prospects, threats of conflict, and actual war—all of which undermine confidence that our children's lives will be better and easier than our own. As we envision our girls facing an even more competitive, rapidly changing, and scarier world, we worry about whether they have whatever it will take for them to become successful. Naturally, many of us are also increasingly confused about what we should be doing to help.

This anxiety often drives parents' hopes and expectations. Many of us begin to look for certain accomplishments—and the sooner the better—so we can be more assured of our daughters' success at the finish line. As a result, however, with their heightened sensitivity to the opinions and perceptions of others, girls often grow up feeling as if every grade, invitation, score, and win was scrutinized. This, of course, adds immeasurably to their own worries about whether they are good enough.

Opportunities Equal Obligations

Thanks to the women's movement; Title IX; and new science, math, and computer programs, the last decade has significantly equalized educational opportunities for girls. And they are taking full advantage. For example, a 2003 *BusinessWeek* cover story reported that girls are now surpassing boys in academic honors, leadership positions, student activity posts, and even team sports. Girls are also outperforming boys in reading, catching up in math, and earning the majority of both bachelor's and master's degrees. In my study, they were almost twice as likely as boys to describe their academic success as "very good" or "excellent." But girls are paying dearly.

Along with a wider range of opportunities and choices comes more pressure. Girls usually see opened doors not as possibilities, but as obligations. That is because they think that if they *can* do something, they *should* do it. Ironically, teens today perceive themselves as having not more choices, but fewer. As Rita explained:

> It used to be that there was only pressure on girls to be popular, pretty, and nice. But now that girls have broken into sports, math, and science, we are expected to be popular, pretty, nice, athletic, and smart. If we fall short on any of these qualities, suddenly we're inadequate. The trouble isn't coming from our minds, it's coming from the world we live in.

The Bar Is Raised

With contemporary culture raising the bar on standards for achievement—academic, extracurricular, and social—girls today think that doing their best just doesn't cut it anymore. Schools, for example, are instilling this belief by accelerating curricula. As Nikki wrote in an e-mail: "School seems much more different right now than a couple of years ago. The district is putting way too much pressure on students. I am in honors math in middle school, and the stuff I'm learning right now in seventh grade my brother learned in his honors class in eighth grade and my dad learned in ninth!"

If your daughter complains about having too much work, she may have valid reasons. Schools are assigning far more homework than in the past. According to the Institute for Social Research at the University of Michigan, from 1981 to 1997 nine- to twelve-year-old children spent 28 percent more time studying. In these same years, the amount of homework assigned to elementary school children tripled. Not surprisingly, the majority of middle school girls I surveyed report they have "too much" or "way too much" homework.

Katie, who is only eleven, wrote in an e-mail, "My life consists of sleeping, eating, school, and homework. Homework is taking over my life. Sometimes I feel like quitting." Shelley says, "My parents have a rule that you have to do your homework first. In the winter, if you spend an hour on it, it gets dark so you can't go out. The pressure is on, and I'm only ten!"

As a result, many of our daughters already feel burned out by the teen years. In high school, two thirds of the girls I surveyed—about 12 percent more than boys—say they feel overwhelmed by homework. Harris Cooper, a professor at the University of Missouri who studies the history of homework, believes that we are now at the peak of a thirty-year upward cycle that is about to reverse. Until then, however, stressed-out girls will undoubtedly continue to tackle piles of homework. The chapters ahead will discuss the various ways that families deal with the when, where, and how of homework.

Excel in Everything

As if curriculum changes aren't enough, our girls are also confronting soaring expectations for extracurricular accomplishments. A school administrator who is about to retire told me, "In my era, we used to be satisfied with a lot less. I screeched away horribly on a cello in the school orchestra. Parents didn't even come to concerts because they were dreadful. Now it's not enough for girls to play in the school orchestra. Now they have to be chosen for a larger orchestra, like the city youth symphony."

This drive for excellence permeates all activities, intimidating girls into avoiding new avenues because they fear they lack extraordinary talent. For example, many girls believe they are not good enough to audition for school plays or special choirs unless they have taken voice, dance, or acting lessons. Maxine, a freshman, says, "There's no way I'm gonna get picked for a good part in the musical, not in my school. Some kids have their own voice coaches, or they've danced in the Nutcracker since they were three. I'm way behind."

In the past, sports offered an enjoyable, healthy outlet for kids. These days, however, being an athlete in middle school or high school has become serious business, more apt to heighten than to reduce stress. Too often girls are burdened by anxiety-ridden tryouts for competitive leagues and premier teams and, if they make teams, multiple practices and games during the week. For too many, the hope of being discovered by talent scouts or recruited by colleges brings on the added pressure of constantly having to prove themselves. In this competitive atmosphere, what happens to the girls who may not be naturally athletic but just enjoy the experience of playing a sport or being part of a team?

The girls in my focus groups often raised this very issue. It was late September, a few weeks into the fall sports schedule at a large, independent high school. Though only a few games had been played, judgments already had been made about various players' relative merits. Not once did the girls speak of having fun or the excitement of a close game or the camaraderie of their teams. Instead, they described with some urgency the pressures of not being good enough, fears of disappointing their parents and teammates, and the prospect of humiliating themselves in the process.

"You can't just do something. You have to be good at it," said Kelilah. "You have to have your coach call home and say, 'Your daughter has real potential and is going to go far.'"

"Yeah," Abby said, "You have lots of pressure on you if you're playing on a school team. You always want to do good and show everyone that you're trying your best."

"It's true," agreed Syd, "I worry about this stuff too when I go to camp. I don't want to be on a team and have everyone be, like, 'Oh no, Syd is in. Let's hope she doesn't mess up. Don't pass to her!'"

Jessi, who had been sitting quietly doing some homework, looked up and said, "People who make teams are so good, it's embarrassing. I'm not athletic, so I run at home. If I can't be good at something, I'm not going to do it."

Whether challenges are academic or extracurricular, the pressure is on. Some girls who believe they lack talent or skill simply try harder. With the drive and discipline of professional dancers, they twist themselves into pretzels with the hope of distinguishing themselves. Cory is a prime example. "I specialize in ballet," she told me, "and that's a lot of pressure because everything needs to be perfect: your body, technique, and musicality. The perfect body proportions are skinny, long legs and arms, a shorter midsection, toes that go straight across, and a good turnout. And the problem is that there are lots of people not born like that, so we have to work twice as hard."

This mentality is not unusual. When parents see daughters committed to their activities, they assume girls are having fun. However, those who are not emotionally ready to handle challenges and disappointments tend to blame themselves if they don't shine. Many are self-conscious about their supposed flaws. This nervous energy is only intensified when coaches, communities, and parents become intensely invested in how well girls do in extracurricular endeavors.

As CJ told me, "I hate hearing, 'You're not trying hard enough. You're not applying yourself!' That's so not true. I keep at it, practicing nonstop, doing all the clinics they want me to do." Although parents think they are just being helpful and encouraging, this sort of involvement backfires. What girls like CJ hear, once again, is that they are not good enough. Her self-esteem suffers because she feels not only misunderstood, but also unaccepted for who she is: a girl who is not the caliber of athlete her parents would like. "What my parents don't get is that no matter how hard I try, I'm not gonna be good! And that," she said sadly, "is not okay with them."

Much to the surprise of their parents, girls who are overwhelmed by pressures to do everything and to do everything well suddenly quit the activities they used to love. Often, teens lose interest in riding or softball or karate, despite years of investment and scores of trophies. But even this decision exacts a toll. With this culture's emphasis on achievement, many girls are ashamed to admit to having limitations. Even when they say, "I can't do everything," teens are not so much accepting reality as apologizing.

Also, girls equate busyness with success. Rushing from volleyball practice to dance class to math and SAT tutors to sleepovers or parties reassures them that they are progressing in all the right areas. Empty spaces in their agendas, therefore, make them uneasy. About 20 to 30 percent of girls believe their involvement in extracurricular activities is "not enough" or "not nearly enough." For these teens, keeping busy may be stressful, but it is a powerful antidote to self-doubt. Still other girls worry about jeopardizing their future success ("What if I could get really good and win competitions?") or feel guilty about the possibility of upsetting and disappointing devoted teachers and supportive parents ("They've paid lots of money for my lessons, and I don't want to make my coach feel bad").

There is also a distinct subset of teens whose pressures in extracurricular areas progressively detach them from their inner lives. These girls follow packed schedules as if on autopilot, numb to whether they are getting anything from their activities—and the cost of their participation. If they pay attention to the inner voices alerting them to their real desires, they risk disappointing or angering adults. The trouble is, if girls continue to ignore these powerful assertions of their real selves, over time they fade away.

GETTING INTO COLLEGE

Looming over girls and exacerbating these everyday pressures is the idea of applying to college. For many, the colleges from which they get acceptance letters will be the ultimate measure of their success. Lanie, a junior in high school, describes the mind-set of many older teens: "This whole year I have so much work to do and I have to worry about keeping my grades up for college. College worries me so much that I almost get physically sick when I think about it. I've been a zombie."

With the rising population of well-prepared students, competition for college has been intensifying every year. Many admissions officers have been quoted as saying they could fill each incoming class many times over with perfectly qualified applicants. Parents and educators are well aware that the college situation is nothing like it used to be. In fact, many college-educated parents believe that if we were applying today, we would probably be rejected from our own alma maters.

Pressure to get into a good school is no longer the exclusive burden of the privileged or those students intent upon elite institutions. While socioeconomic factors play a role in college pressure, they don't tell the whole story. Having affluent or accomplished parents can make it harder for daughters trying to follow in their footsteps. But coming from a more modest background does not ensure immunity. Ambitious girls who lack financial means are often determined to excel to justify their parents' hard work and sacrifices. They are also motivated to earn scholarships.

Perhaps to cope with the pressure and avoid potential rejection, some girls purposely or unconsciously aim low—that is, they apply to colleges for which they are overqualified. Those who aim high usually find senior year extraordinarily stressful. In my experience, the narrower and more elite a girl or her parents set the sights for college and the more they succumb to the accompanying cultural pressures, the greater the entire family's distress. Girls who seem relatively spared from college-induced anxiety usually see a broad range of options, have fairly solid qualifications, and also have parents who share their views.

It Starts Earlier

Girls are also more stressed out today because the hype about college is starting long before it used to. This story is typical. The summer before their son's senior year of high school, my friends began taking him around to visit colleges. As one tour began, the student guide asked potential applicants to state their name, high school, and grade. One by one, they did as he asked. Finally, everyone turned expectantly to the remaining student, a girl who had been feverishly filling pages in a spiral notebook. "Sandra," she said. "Westville. Freshman." The incredulous student guide blurted, "In high school?"

This would-be early applicant is not alone. By middle school, one third of girls say they "usually" or "always" worry about getting into the "right" college. Even many *Girls' Life* readers, who are under age fourteen, have formed rather specific and, most likely, premature goals. Their stress is almost palpable:

+ "I don't know what I want to do, but I definitely want to go to Stanford, Princeton, or Duke. My parents told me about those colleges."

+ "I want to go to Juilliard to study music, and that college doesn't let just anyone in. The more I started thinking about this, the more I started freaking out about getting straight A's. Everything started suffering—my relationships, my physical condition."

+ "After I got a bad grade, that's when I started to pressure myself to get better grades or else not get into veterinarian school when I get older."

As a result, school personnel are dealing with more and more nervous kids and their parents. Recently I asked the psychologist of a small independent school when her students typically begin to feel pressured. "Well . . . ," she said. "When they're born? I have to remind parents and kids that middle school grades don't count for college. But I'm never sure they believe me." My talks with girls suggest that she is absolutely right.

Making the Grades

With increased competition for college, many high schools impress upon their students—from the time they enter the doors as freshmen—the importance of their academic records. In doing so, however, they ratchet up the pressure. Graciella, who attended one of my focus groups, reported, "They are always bringing it up to us, from the first day of high school. At orientation they tell us that colleges look at all four years of your high school record. And they never stop telling us."

Now add taking the SATs, which teens invariably see as the event determining their future success. Convinced that a few points in either direction will make or break them, these standardized tests usually raise girls' anxiety to the max. As Jan expressed in a focus group, "I was never so nervous in my entire life. Knowing that whichever circles I filled in would totally decide my future. I knew if I did bad, it could literally ruin my life."

All too often I hear of girls crying, withdrawing, resenting their more successful friends, and denigrating themselves when they receive their SAT scores. The fact that scores are so public exacerbates their fears of being exposed. Make no mistake about this: Nearly every junior or senior girl can rattle off the verbal, math, and combined SAT scores of their classmates. Many believe these numbers define them and exactly where they stand in relation to everyone else. As Natalie told me, "I do pretty well in school. I make honor roll and stuff. But I feel really stupid because my friends all broke 1500!"

The hype about grades and scores puts parents in a bind. On some level everyone knows test scores are just numbers, not a reflection of who our daughters really are. And yet the reality is that these numbers do matter. Because we want our girls to be as successful as possible, we cannot help but worry. But it is how we manage our anxiety that counts. Above all, we want to avoid adding to our daughters' own worries. Anna says, rolling her eyes, "My parents say every single grade counts toward my future. Everything I do now." In a voice laced with sarcasm, she adds, "Not *too* much pressure!"

The quandary for many parents is how far to go to help. When is it appropriate to prepare girls? How much intervention is useful? Although many parents are unable to afford or are philosophically opposed to the explosive industry of SAT courses and tutoring programs, some of us end up capitulating and signing up our daughters. We think it isn't fair to our girls to deprive them of an advantage that everyone else seems to be getting. Essentially, we give in to cultural pressure in the hope of keeping level the playing field. What we fear most of all is not doing right by our children.

It is easy to overlook the potential drawbacks of all this intervention, the subtle messages inherent in "marketing" our children. The truth is, many girls say they are more stressed by such efforts to help and resent the extra burden costly programs place upon them. "My parents have me going to all these people who are supposed to help me get into a fabulous college," Melanie told our group. "I don't have time to breathe!" Claire said, "My mom thinks I should give up my entire social life so I can get into a good college. She doesn't let me go to parties because I have a tutor on Friday nights."

Claire's experience is not universal, but it is far from uncommon. With college-related anxiety rising exponentially throughout high school, parents bend over backward to give their daughters every opportunity to develop all of their potential assets. As Judith R. Shapiro, the president of Barnard College, in New York City, has said, "Parents attuned to the barrage of media coverage believe that the best colleges accept only superhumans . . . and strive to prepare their sons and daughters accordingly."

The Quest for Angularity

Teen girls also get the message from this culture that they should find at least one area in which they can stand out. By age fourteen or sixteen or eighteen, they believe they have to specialize. Being well rounded is no longer enough. "My parents define success as good grades," reported Yinuo, a diminutive Asian student in an independent girls' school. "But also I have to stand out in extracurricular activities. I want to experience different things, but my parents think I should choose only one thing—"

"Me too!" interrupted Sasha. "I prefer a taste of life rather than dedicating myself to one thing. I'd feel like I'm missing too much. I think I'm getting good experiences when I try out for a club or try piano or dance. But now that I'm in high school, there's pressure to focus on one thing. It's a college thing."

Not too long ago I attended a seminar in my own community that promoted this unfortunate perspective. Offered by well-known educational consultants and entitled "Reducing the Stress Associated with the College Application Process," their basic message was that students aspiring to elite colleges needed to be "angular." That is, they had to stand out in some way—as artists, musicians, writers, athletes, or leaders. Applicants were to avoid being "serial joiners," the term sometimes used to describe students who participate in many clubs and activities but don't assume leadership roles.

One mother attending this lecture bravely voiced what many other parents were undoubtedly thinking: "But my daughter is kind of an all-around good student . . ." There was an audible hum as parents murmured, waiting for expert words of reassurance. The senior consultant's reply, "There are other colleges, you know, besides the Ivies," caused a collective hush to settle over the room. In this town, at least, nervous energy had hit new heights.

During a focus group I asked the junior girls sitting around the table this very question: "What if you're not great at any one thing right now?" Before they uttered a single word, their groans and sagging shoulders had spoken volumes.

"I really need a goal in life," lamented Lana, a soft-spoken girl. "I don't know what I want to be and I'm trying to decide. I'm trying to be okay with that."

"I find that I have that pressure too," Monica chimed in. "I may be good at a bunch of things, but there's nothing I excel at." There was silence for a moment, and then she got to the crux of the issue. "The thing is," she mused, "*poorly* well-rounded doesn't matter." With this belief, what teen wouldn't teeter on the way to success?

SOCIAL PRESSURES

Along with the pressures of excelling in academics and activities, this culture further burdens girls. The signals about what it takes to be a desirable young woman today are notoriously confusing— and sometimes even contradictory. For girls in middle school and high school, the path to social success is often a confusing jumble of unmarked roads and hairpin turns. This is a climate that breeds self-doubt.

Speaking to an assembly of girls, I begin by asking what they find most challenging about high school. Instantly there is a flurry of hands in the air. Expecting to hear about homework, tests, schedules, and other relatively impersonal topics, I am surprised when Diane, a fourteen-year-old freshman, speaks about pressing social demands:

You get all this pressure from the girls you go to school with or a
boyfriend if you're lucky to have one. They want you to be
pretty, sweet, and skinny, but they don't want anybody else to see
you that way. Then you also have to be beautiful to be popular.
If you're not popular, then you have little chance to be noticed.

These words are like a call to arms. Diane's words opened the
floodgates; scores of hands are suddenly waving vigorously in the
air. Sooner or later, this same scenario unfolds in every school I
visit, and I hear remarkably similar themes about what it takes to
be socially successful. Walking the tightrope, girls try to avoid
falling into one of two equally undesirable abysses: On the one
hand, if they're not enough, they're failures; on the other hand, if
they're too much, they arouse the envy of competitive peers and
thereby risk rejection.

Media Messages

The impact of the media on teenage girls and their self-image has
been a hot topic in both the news and professional literature. As
everyone knows, teen girls are bombarded with images in magazines, in films, and on television that portray ultrathin, sexy young
women with flawless skin and perfect hair. Usually, they are posed
with attractive, attentive young men and surrounded by cultural
symbols of success.

My survey mirrors research data on this subject, which says that
some girls are affected and others are not. Although two thirds of
middle school girls and three fourths of high school girls completing my survey say they "rarely" or "never" feel pressured by the media, 7 percent of middle schoolers and 15 percent of high schoolers
do say they "usually" or "always" experience this sort of pressure.

After I spoke at thirteen-year-old Trudy's school, she sent an e-mail that described how the media adds to her other pressures of trying to measure up:

> *I think that there is so much pressure for girls to be perfect now. You have the media with all those super skinny girls with perfect hair and make-up and clothes, and you have those snotty girls in school that tease you if you don't wear what they wear. I feel like there is so much expected of me with my friends, family, teachers, and coaches. It's terrible. It's way hard to keep up with all of the pressure.*

Conducting focus groups in middle schools, I learned more about what young teens think about how television, movies, and magazines portray them. One of them, an attractive girl on the verge of puberty, comments, "You see all these perfect people on TV who have a perfect job and perfect body. You say to yourself, 'To get there, I have to be like that.'"

"Yeah," replies her friend Marcella. "TV shows someone's idea of a normal person—a thin, pretty girl with friends who never talk behind her back, loving parents behind her in everything she does, and boys falling all over her. It makes a lot of girls think, 'If I'm not like that, how am I going to make it?' This all leads to low self-esteem."

Kellie then says, "You look in a magazine and think that's what girls are supposed to look like. Then when you wake up in the morning and your hair is all over the place and you have a big zit on your face, of course you think you're ugly."

Yet, ironically, these observations somehow empower the girls. It is as if hearing their thoughts out loud prompts them to counteract these harmful media messages, perhaps to protest that they are not naive, helpless victims of the media. They become invested in proving that they know better than to believe everything they read in teen magazines or see on TV and in the movies.

"They never tell you everything that the model had to go through just to look like that," Amanda says. "She may not even look like that in real life."

"That's right," adds another middle schooler. "I read in a magazine once about how many hours models have to sit there totally bored while hair people and makeup people do what they're supposed to. They dyed this model's hair and eyelashes, put this stuff all over her skin, and did all kinds of things to her so she'd look good."

"I think I heard that too," says her friend. "They interviewed models to find out all the tricks. And even after all of that, they just airbrush pictures if there's even one teensy spot on their skin."

After reassuring themselves with these facts, the girls are all smiles, as if the media has suddenly become a far less credible and persuasive source of information about what they should be striving for. Knowing how the entertainment and fashion industries perform their tricks, they are no longer so awed or impressed by the magic. Such discussions with girls reaffirmed my belief that they need our encouragement to critically evaluate—and counteract—the destructive messages they get from this culture.

Appearance Counts

Still, it is an understatement that many teen girls are preoccupied with their appearance. Unlike boys, they often spend their school nights casing their wardrobes, strategically planning their outfits, and worrying about whether they will inadvertently appear too something—too fat, too revealing, too babyish, too out of style, too out there, and so on. Though she just started middle school, Lauren has already identified the quandary common to so many teens: "I think there is confusion about how much makeup you should wear and how short your skirt should be without being a tramp. Pressure to be not too goody-goody also comes from peers in school."

Her best friend, Michele, adds, "Most people don't even care how boys look, but they call girls who show too much skin a slut or whore. And they think that all girls think about is boys and gossip. So to avoid these labels, girls try to be perfect. But usually they're misunderstood and called 'teacher's pet' or 'stuck up.' I know I feel more pressured than I ever did before."

Trying desperately to read and conform to these confusing cultural messages, girls spend precious minutes—and sometimes hours, parents tell me—before school every morning blow-drying their hair and either straightening or curling it, depending upon their idea of perfection. They worry whether their eye shadow is too light, too dark, too glittery, or just too much. Even picking out jeans is often stressful. Beyond designer or brand, girls know that whether they wear pencil cut, slim fit, boot cut, low rise, superlow rise, frayed, stretch, long fit, lean fit, reverse fit, loose fit, classic fit, or flare jeans telegraphs to their peers something crucial about who they are. Advertisers exploit adolescent insecurity by making sure girls are well aware of this.

For girls trying to conform to this unwritten formula for the perfect appearance, the list of potential transgressions grows as they do. As a result, the most socially ambitious teenage girls today are expending enormous energy figuring out how to walk impossibly thin lines. The most resilient are able to manage these pressures well enough, with minimal effect on their emotional well-being and general productivity.

For many girls, however, this level of expectation proves too much to bear. The reason, I believe, is clear. Without sufficient understanding and support, many girls eventually succumb to simultaneous cultural pressures to excel academically, to be everything to everyone, to find their one or two outstanding talents, and to look perfect.

OVERWHELMED GIRLS

Girls who internalize this impossible recipe for success unwittingly set themselves up for overwhelming stress, if not failure. It is nerve-racking to walk a tightrope when even one misstep could be disastrous. They are in a chronic state of imbalance. The belief that they are not and might never be good enough, or that they are one step away from disaster, undermines our daughters' self-confidence and insidiously estranges them from their inner lives.

Of all the girls I have spoken with, I think Shari most poignantly expressed the toll of cultural pressures. During a focus group she said:

> *Us girls today do our best and we want to be the greatest. We try hard to please our family and friends, and we know that our family and friends are very proud of us. But we are always thinking that something is missing, like are we being the greatest friend in the world? Are we doing the best to achieve our goals? Are we reaching high enough for the stars?*

Shari's adviser, who had been sitting nearby at her desk, suddenly looked up. With a disconcerted look, Mrs. Farrell said, "You know, I have a ten-year-old daughter, and I think she's already feeling like this. Very often something at school makes her cry. She says, 'I didn't do X well enough.'" Mrs. Farrell added wistfully, "What is that going to do to her little personality? She never feels like she's good enough."

It was apparent to everyone in the room that Shari's words had prompted this teacher to think about her own daughter's behavior in a new way. This is not surprising. It is usually hard for adults to know how much girls are really suffering until they are made aware of a crisis—or at least the threat of one.

This is precisely what happened with Stefanie, a capable middle schooler whose mother brought her to me for therapy. Her concern was Stefanie's outbursts of temper, which were not only increasing in frequency, but also disrupting and frightening her family. At the slightest provocation, it seemed, she would "go ballistic," screaming at whoever angered her. This bewildered her mother because Stefanie was the epitome of an accomplished eighth grader: She excelled in school, was a fabulous athlete, had a circle of close friends, and played a mean trumpet.

At first glance, Stefanie was lively and remarkably poised in her uniform of fashion-conscious but conservative younger teens; her huge brown eyes sparkled whenever she smiled. Highly articulate, she eagerly rattled off her activities: ballet, confirmation class, volunteering at a shelter, field hockey, and, since the previous week, playing in a jazz ensemble. She told me, "I get pretty good grades and I always do my work. I like being involved, and I love it when my teachers say they wish they had more kids like me." It was only Stefanie's body language that hinted of brewing tension; she sat restlessly at the edge of her chair, one foot tapping constantly against the floor.

Over time Stefanie opened up, revealing just how unhappy and overwhelmed she really felt beneath a veneer of perkiness and competence. Finally voicing thoughts and feelings that had long been pent up, her words often tumbled out in a breathless torrent. "There's no way to explain all the stress. I'm more worried about grades every minute than learning the material. I can't get everything done and do it right," she said. "At night, I always stay awake thinking of all I have to do. Sometimes I wake up in the middle of the night and do it." By now, she is angrily brushing tears from her eyes. "There really aren't enough hours in the day. The stress is like falling down a big hole."

Seeing her exemplary report cards, Stefanie's parents assumed school was going well. But learning had become torture. She began to dread getting back quizzes, papers, and tests because of what scores had come to mean. "The grade won't lie," Stefanie told me. "It compares me to other kids, and to myself." Getting a B minus on a math test nearly devastated her. "My teacher said this stuff wasn't going to be on the test and it was. It's so unfair! I used to have an A average, but now, forget it."

In her mind, this one disappointing math grade defined her. Good grades in other subjects no longer cheered her up. Like many teens I have gotten to know, Stefanie began to think of herself as an impostor. Inside she felt nothing like the successful girl other people saw when they looked at her. More and more she felt empty and disconnected from herself.

Through therapy, Stefanie realized that her ability to cope had frayed. She was going through her days feeling irritable, defeated, and, sometimes, hopeless. In fact, she related this telling incident. Returning from an all-day field trip, she was sitting next to her best friend on the school bus when "an annoying boy kept kicking our seat. It was driving me absolutely crazy. My friend could've cared less. I got fed up and turned around and gave him hell. But then my friend asked me why I was so mean." She looked at me intently as she asked, "Why did his kicking bother me and not Bethany?"

Most of the time Stefanie succeeded in containing her anxiety, frustration, and anger at school. Her teachers saw her as angelic. But by the end of the day, she had had it. In the relative safety of her home, Stefanie could let down her guard and reveal her distress. She reported a rather classic family scenario: "When I got home, I sat down on my floor and I just couldn't move. Then my mother came in and asked why I wasn't being 'productive.' Sometimes stress can make me really snappy. I have no patience at all. So I yell at my sister or my mom."

Stefanie and her parents came to see that her outbursts were the most outward sign that her balance was faltering. Conforming to expectations to excel in everything, and with her self-regard sinking by the day, Stefanie told me, "Sometimes I really feel I am not good enough for people."

When her parents became aware of her struggles, they gave her the gift of a safety net before she toppled into a full-blown crisis. As she became clearer about her needs, she was able to ask more appropriately for help. In the short run, she used practical strategies to relieve her stress: she got help to stay better organized, worked with a supportive math tutor, and made her schedule less hectic. Over time, Stefanie was able to make inner changes as well, such as relaxing her overly rigid standards.

But other girls struggle silently with similar stressful cultural messages about success, delaying or never getting the help that could alleviate their distress and strengthen their confidence. A few, like Stefanie, become overwhelmed and yet hesitate to reveal their pain and ask for support from their families.

The next chapter will give you a closer look into the family situations that typically compound the cultural pressures on girls to be successful and affect whether or not they speak up and get the support they need. Some may be familiar, others not. Some you can fix; others you can't control. Yet it is important to appreciate how family dynamics can powerfully influence your daughter's perceptions of herself and her own success.

CHAPTER 3

Proving Themselves: Family Dynamics

Despite our best intentions, certain family dynamics seem to exaggerate our daughters' nervous energy around achievement. Without a doubt, girls look to their parents and siblings to gauge what is expected of them. They learn from what we say, what we do, what we don't say or do, and what we model just by living our lives.

This is not to say that we should accept all the blame if our daughters mess up—or take all the credit if they shine. Obviously, we don't have *that* much control; innate intelligence, opportunity, temperament, education, life events, and chance factors do play a role in how girls turn out. But as any teen will tell you, family pressures loom large in shaping how she thinks of herself and her success.

A girl's birth order, for example, largely determines the family into which she is born. Relative to siblings who come before or after her, she may have parents who are at different points in their marriages and careers. She may or may not have brothers or sisters to whom she can compare herself. As discussed later in this chapter, whether her siblings are older or younger, of the same or different gender, and the age gap between them, all these factors enormously influence her experience of herself in the world. You can't change your family's constellation. It is what it is. But it is vital to recognize the power of these dynamics.

Since girls generally want to conform to their families' standards, their perceptions of what their parents want them to accomplish can add immeasurably to the pressure they feel to be successful. When they are already stressed out, family issues are often the proverbial straw that tips them into crisis. This is especially true for teens who are already distracted by pressing personal or family problems, but family dynamics play into other vulnerabilities and tax girls in predictable ways.

For teens in transition, for example, starting a new school provides ready-made benchmarks for comparisons with siblings. Teachers unwittingly contribute by comparing girls to their older brothers and sisters, and sometimes even prejudging them according to their siblings' track records. Girls then feel even greater pressure to measure up—or to carve out different roles. Unlike socially confident teens, insecure girls who crave peer acceptance usually need more affirmation and support from their parents and siblings. When family dynamics are also stressful, these girls are that much more likely to suffer.

Perfectionistic girls, who are characteristically exacting of themselves, are highly sensitive to perceived criticism. Parents must be scrupulously aware of what these girls assume about family expectations and demands in order to correct misconceptions and ease their intense pressure. Girls who already feel like square pegs because they are different from their peers, parents, or siblings are extremely affected by any family dynamics that make them further question their value.

Your daughter, ever on the lookout for cues about her status in her family, is keenly attuned to everyone else's accomplishments and failures. She makes all sorts of assumptions about where she fits in, what you expect of her, and whether she can ever measure up. You don't have to say a single word. Clara, for example, explained why she feels inferior to her brother: "It's not like my parents actually said, 'We want you to be just like James. He's smart, he gets good grades, and he got into a great college.' But that's exactly what they think." You might wonder whether your daughter, too, is operating under these or similar presumptions.

Families have the potential either to inflame or to reduce girls' stress about achievement. Yet it is easy for parents to overlook their impact until a crisis erupts. Loren's mother and father were caught unawares. A while back, I was asked to see this bright, lively seventeen-year-old girl whose persistent underachievement mystified everyone. To get a clearer picture of Loren's strengths and weaknesses, as well as the reasons for her predicament, I gave her a full battery of cognitive, academic, and personality tests.

Among them was the Thematic Apperception Test (TAT), a widely used storytelling technique that uses ambiguous pictures to evoke attitudes, hopes, aspirations, difficulties, and problem-solving approaches. This was Loren's response to the first picture, a boy looking down at a violin, which typically elicits themes of achievement:

> *A little boy's parents bought him a violin because they wanted him to learn how to play it. So they bought him a nice one, hired a good teacher, and all without telling him first. When he found out, he wasn't happy about it because he had no interest or passion in learning to play the violin. But his parents just talked about how they had already spent the money and how he would learn to appreciate having the skill later in life. So every day they set aside half an hour for him to practice and he's sitting there bored and unhappy, wishing he was doing something else.*

Loren's story, of course, reflected her views of her own family. Like the boy in her story, she believed that her parents had decided what was best for her and made all the necessary arrangements without consulting her. Loren was keenly aware of her parents' investment in her success. She coped with this additional stress by taking the path of least resistance. To avoid confronting her mother and father—and therefore causing trouble—she went through the motions of what they asked. But her heart wasn't in her efforts. Until she felt free to explore what really intrigued and mattered to her, Loren couldn't discover, much less make good use of, her many talents.

To avoid such situations, it is crucial to be aware of the family messages, both spoken and assumed, that your daughter is getting about success. One, if you are sensitive to the thoughts and feelings she may be keeping hidden—from both you and herself—you will ask different questions. Two, if you discover she is harboring misconceptions that are eating away at her sense of self, you can set her straight. Three, if you can empathize with how your daughter sees herself within your family, you will be less likely to inadvertently make matters worse.

For example, had Loren's parents been aware of how negatively she experienced their efforts, they might have rethought their approach, enlisted her input in making decisions, and avoided alienating her. Had they imagined what she was thinking, they might have clarified what they really expected of her. Most of all, had they known about Loren's basic need to figure out her own interests and passions, they might have asked the sorts of questions that inspire teens to gain insight into themselves. These strategies could well have prevented Loren from turning off to school.

Regardless of whether your own daughter is coping well or struggling at this moment, it will help you to be informed about the most common family dynamics that contribute to—or exacerbate—achievement-related stress.

SIBLINGS

Although sibling dynamics are varied and extraordinarily complex, what I have learned from girls can be summarized rather simply: They feel as if they can't win. What I mean is, it matters little whether teens are oldest, middle, or only children. Whatever their family position, they take on a certain set of ambitions and expectations, all of which add exponentially to their pressure for success. Whether they are motivated by the desire to compete, to compensate, or to champion, girls who look at their families and feel the need to prove themselves are more stressed than those who don't.

Competing with Superstars

In the most common scenario, girls feel competitive with brothers and sisters whom they perceive as more talented than they are. Teens often tell me it is frustrating when siblings are so smart, popular, athletic, or musical that they are impossible to emulate—and the accomplishments of these superstar siblings seem to come too easily. Of course, comparing themselves constantly and unfavorably to such alleged paragons of success intensifies stressed-out girls' feelings of inadequacy.

The closer in age to their idealized siblings, the more girls feel compelled to follow in their exalted footsteps. And, as many parents have experienced, the stronger identification of same-sex siblings makes the competition between sisters especially dicey. Imagine how girls suffer when their younger siblings catch up to them in skills and accomplishments—or, worse, when they leave them in the dust.

Girls rarely voice these feelings. It is only their behavior at home—perhaps picking on siblings, being nasty, or instigating conflict—that tips off their families to their underlying distress. Unless teachers and parents are alert to girls' sensitivity about being undervalued in their families or inferior to their siblings, even casual comments can accidentally rub salt in their wounds. As Diana told me, "Every time I get a new teacher, they do the same thing. They ask me if I'm Terry's younger sister. And when I say I am, they ask me if I'm just as smart. Or they say they're happy I'm in their class, like they're expecting me to be amazing, too. It makes me so mad."

You may view your daughter's sibling situation as a given, perhaps something she should just accept and get over. But it is important not to underestimate how intense feelings about brothers and sisters can be—and how forcefully they can shape your daughter's growing sense of self. When the high school students in my focus group broached this topic one morning, I was taken aback by the emotion driving their words.

"I feel like I had to be perfect for a long time. My brother is so much smarter than me," says Valerie. "In fifth grade he tested at the college level for math. He's also in the top ten in the country for swimming. I feel I have a lot to live up to."

Her friend Katy clearly relates. "My sister was gorgeous. Everybody knew her in high school. I never saw her do any work, and she got into Princeton. My mother expects a lot from me."

How girls come to these conclusions—and whether or not they are accurately reading their parents—is a complex issue. Teasing out everyone's perceptions is like untangling a skein of yarn. For example, a *Girls' Life* reader asked in an e-mail, "What do I do when I get yelled at for getting a bad grade because I am not as smart as my siblings?" Are this girl's parents really critical of her for not performing as well as her siblings, or is she distorting the situation? Does she truly feel out of her league in her family, much like a square peg? Or is she focusing on her more highly achieving siblings to avoid taking responsibility for her own disappointing work?

In a perfect world, mothers and fathers know not to compare their kids. But that is one of the directives from parenting experts that is easier said than done. In fact, it is hard to imagine having more than one child and *not* using one's experiences as a frame of reference for another. The real problem is using a cookie-cutter approach to raising kids—that is, trying to make all children turn out exactly the same. Growing up with parents who have this goal convinces girls that there is only one way to be: just like their siblings. If they are different, teens believe they are not measuring up. This is true of Kendra, who becomes tearful while discussing her family:

> *All my sisters went to graduate school, and my parents expect me to go to graduate school. It's the prestige. They always want something good, what they see as excellent and best, because of their past experiences and friends. In order to be successful, you need to try your hardest and get good grades. You want to live up to their expectations.*

Kendra has internalized her parents' high standards. They want the best for her. You might be wondering what could be wrong with that. Well, like many girls who don't want to follow the family script—or who believe they aren't capable of doing so—Kendra hides her misery beneath dutiful behavior. "I don't necessarily want to go to graduate school," she confesses. The price of her decision? "I'll be the less important daughter, the less important sister. I know it's not good to compare." Kendra's self-deprecation is obvious to everyone in the room.

I frequently hear stories with similar themes. Mia says, "Just because my brother had no social life in high school and stayed home studying every Friday and Saturday night, my parents think there's something wrong with me if I want to go out with my friends." Beth Ann tells me, "My sister and my mom are really, really close. My sister tells my mom everything, so my mom thinks I should too. She gets all mad or worried when I don't like to tell her stuff, but I just like my privacy."

As you consider your own family dynamics, remember that girls may or may not perceive their siblings the way you do as the parent. Maybe you can't deny that your teen is hard pressed to fill the shoes of an extraordinary brother or sister. Or you might think she is exaggerating, even idealizing, her sibling's accomplishments. Either way, as you think about how to ease her competitive feelings, these suggestions may be helpful.

First, be assured that no matter how hard you try, you can't completely eliminate sibling rivalry. Second, even if you could, it would probably be unwise. Competing with brothers and sisters has its benefits. Girls who learn to handle competitive relationships within their families are better prepared to do so later on with roommates, colleagues, friends, and coworkers.

Having said that, it is still important to make sure you are not fueling your daughter's rivalry with her siblings. No parent is perfect. So do some honest soul searching. If your daughter complains that you compare her too much to her successful siblings, could she be right? Is she possibly keying into feelings that have been outside your awareness? For example, is it okay for your children to carve their own path, or do you envision a specific route to success in your family? Has a particular expectation been around for generations?

If you answered yes to any of these questions, be kind to yourself. This realization can be the first step in relieving your daughter's distress. Besides, it is natural to want *all* of your children to succeed. Most parents would prefer kids to be responsible and self-motivated, to remember to do their work, and to do well in school. These girls are easier to raise. And when one child's troubles claim a disproportionate share of parental attention and energy, it is hard on everyone else in the family.

If you believe the competition among your children is destructive, find ways to take the edge off. Parents with twins often deal with this issue. Recently, for example, I worked with Alicia, the mother of twelve-year-old girls. Lydia, athletic and outgoing, made dozens of new friends within weeks of starting middle school. Although she did well enough in class, academics were not her priority. Sophie, on the other hand, was quieter and shied away from coed and large group gatherings. Since she had trouble reading in the earlier grades, she learned to give schoolwork her full attention. Sophie's extra efforts to be organized and use diligent work habits were paying dividends in sixth grade.

Lydia and Sophie's long-standing competition intensified in middle school. With their burgeoning self-consciousness, they increasingly looked to each other as the ideal to be achieved. Lydia envied Sophie's academic achievement and Sophie was jealous of Lydia's rapidly expanding social network. Alicia worked hard to defuse this rivalry by supporting each girl's uniqueness. She signed them up for different camps and sports, despite the inevitable schedule conflicts and carpooling nightmares. Alicia explained, "It's bad enough they're always looking at each other and thinking, 'Am I the best?' I don't want them to have to compete on the basketball court or the softball field too."

Finding Their Place

Just as they stress out about their status with friends, teen girls constantly assess where they stand in their families and how they stack up with their brothers and sisters. Of course, what they *really* want to know is whether they are special enough. "Well, I have a junior sister and I'm not the smartest one in the family," says

Lynette, looking sad. "I'm not the best in athletics either. I get the most stress from my mom. I have to be good at something."

You might ask yourself if your daughter is picking up on such subtle, unspoken messages. Do you tend to label your kids on the basis of their accomplishments—or lack thereof? The trouble with this is twofold. One, girls can too easily be pigeonholed in negative ways—for example, the child who is always in trouble, does things at the last minute, hogs the computer or phone, or fights with her parents. Since teen girls are developing, they are still in flux. In the course of discovering who they are, they may try on many different personas. Fixed labels therefore do them a disservice, essentially binding them to identities that may already be a thing of the past—or will be shortly.

Two, when girls are given positive labels—for example, the honors student, the athlete of the family, the hardworking sister, or the one who does her chores perfectly—they often feel compelled to maintain that status. Anna describes, "My sister isn't as good in school as I am, and my parents are always pressuring her to do better. When I hear them, I want to make myself do better at school. The pressure they put on her rubs off on me." When I ask why, she says, "I don't want to disappoint them." Anna fears slipping up and landing smack in her sister's unenviable position in the family.

Could your daughter be hiding self-denigrating attitudes and perceptions brought on by family dynamics? Does she "joke" about being the ditz of the family or the problem child who gives you gray hair? Margaret tells our focus group, "My brother is in law school and doing well. I'm not the best student in high school, but I'm graduating this year. My other sibling is going to be a doctor. He knows what he wants to do. My sister is an amazing writer, and I'm kind of the stupid one." The lighthearted giggle that followed is forced, a flimsy effort to cover up what is surely deeply felt distress.

The Burden of All the Expectations

Even if your daughter's siblings are at the other end of the continuum—that is, poor achievers or troubled in some way—she is not immune to family-induced stress. In fact, these girls often feel equally under the gun to succeed. That is because they take it upon themselves to shine to compensate for their older brothers' or sisters' lack of accomplishment. As Tina tells our focus group, "Education is important in my family. I have two older brothers. Both are smarter than me, but one has Asperger's. I have better study habits and social skills. Because he doesn't have the potential to go to Harvard, it puts more pressure on me."

Andressa explains a similar motivation to succeed. She feels responsible to be a role model for her younger siblings because her older brother, the more likely candidate, abdicated that position. "My older brother didn't go to college. It's already stressful trying to be the first one in the family because my parents came from the Dominican Republic," Andressa says, "but I also have to set an example for my brother and sister. I have to keep trying to make honors every quarter."

Sometimes parents specify their hopes. Other times, girls silently take on the expectations they presume their mothers and fathers have for them. In my experience, most often stress results from a combination of the two. Even if parents are not explicit about their desires, sensitive teens pick up on their unconscious wishes, taking them on in an effort to please them. As Justine, a competitive swimmer who took on the role of her family's best hope for a scholarship, says, "I get the burden of all the expectations."

You might imagine that only children, spared of sibling rivalry, would get a pass on nervous energy. By default, however, they often see themselves as their parents' one and only chance to see a child shine. Girls feel the heat, often without their mothers and fathers having a clue. Hester, for example, declares to the group, "Well, I'm an only child. It adds lots of stress. My parents are trying to raise the perfect child, the ideal child. They have only one shot. And I'm it."

FAMILY LIFESTYLE

What We Model

Parents can also contribute to a daughter's stress about achievement by how we live our lives. Girls get powerful messages about success just from observing us. At this stage of life, kids may see us as stable or thriving in our careers. Unless we deliberately share our war stories, our girls may never learn how we started out, stumbled, suffered setbacks, and paid our dues. It is all too easy for them to think of our accomplishments as quick and effortless. Instead, teens need to appreciate that becoming successful is a long-term process that is usually characterized by fits and starts.

Besides the more visible markers of parents' achievements, girls also pick up on our unspoken feelings about work—the regretted decisions, frustrations, unfulfilled ambitions, and desires. If you are trying to keep all this from your daughter, you may want to reconsider. Though there are few hard and fast rules in psychology, this is one of them: Kids may not know the details, but they always pick up on the gist of whatever information their parents are trying to keep private. And girls, with their fine-tuned antennae, rarely fail to intuit our true feelings.

Teen girls are especially attuned to whether their mothers are content with their lives. What ideas might you be conveying to your daughter? Did you give up a career to raise your children? If you work outside the home, are you doing so by choice? Are you working part time, full time, or overtime? Are you generally content, or are you ambivalent about your decisions? Do you have opinions about what you might have done differently—or what your daughter should do to avoid replicating your situation? Do you believe your daughter should pursue a particular career? Are you invested in seeing her follow a path similar to yours or, conversely, taking a whole different route?

Whether or not women are in the workforce, many stressed-out girls can't help but notice that their mothers' daily lives are as hectic as their own. In addition to child rearing and household duties, many mothers take on an extraordinary number of time-consuming commitments all at once. And many women I know exercise to stay in great shape, cook gourmet meals for their families, and maintain well-organized, attractive homes. If your outlook matches this description of the modern woman, you are essentially modeling for your daughter how to walk a tightrope. Your teen is learning that being a woman entails running around trying to be everything to everyone, with little time to herself, and possibly feeling hopeless about doing anything really well.

The Price of Privilege

Some parents also need to consider the effects of a privileged background on a teen girl's stress. Simply put, it has its pros and cons. If you can afford the best and the most, your daughter might feel pressured to take full advantage of everything offered. Again, opened doors usually usher in more obligations—and, therefore, busier schedules. I will never forget Rochelle, who prided herself on creatively squeezing piano lessons into her middle school daughter's busy schedule. She told me she was paying extra for a prestigious teacher to come to their home—at six o'clock in the morning!

Many affluent families value their kids having a variety of experiences and support them in taking full advantage of their opportunities. But often girls get the message from the time they are young that they are expected to do everything and that they should be able to manage many different demands and commitments. Leah, a bubbly student in one of my high school focus groups, speaks of this predicament:

> *It comes partly from affluence. My parents live in a certain area that's considered good. If I have something to do, like a debate tournament, that's okay, but I should also do my homework while I'm there. I'm always doing two things at once.*

Her friend Deena adds, "My mom wants me to be doing my homework that's due two days from now, then go to tennis, then practice piano, and always be active. She wants me to do fifty million things at the same time." This was a refrain sung by many teen girls, but especially by those from more privileged families.

Another challenge for daughters of successful parents is living up to their ideal. This is nothing new. But girls today have bigger hurdles. Many of our own parents thought we were amazing if we merely went to college. For this generation, getting an undergraduate degree is the minimum expectation of many families. These days, for girls to be considered really successful they have to go on to graduate school or get an advanced degree in law, business, or medicine. In the latest trend, college students are completing two and three majors, just to cover their bases.

Socioeconomically, this is the first generation of young people that often fails to surpass the wage-earning capacity or standard of living achieved by its parents. Many girls know that they cannot afford to buy a home in the communities in which they were raised. On the East Coast, this reality is partly responsible for the number of twenty-somethings returning to their parents after college. Without hope of achieving their dreams and perpetuating the lifestyle in which they grew up, many young women become demoralized and apathetic, with predictable effects on their self-esteem.

This was the case with Naomi, a twenty-two-year-old young woman who came for therapy because she was dissatisfied with her life. She facetiously described herself as "going nowhere fast." Having grown up in an affluent suburb, the daughter of a high-level corporate executive and a housewife, Naomi had enjoyed a comfortable lifestyle but an unhappy childhood. She was well aware of her parents' marital troubles and discontent. After briefly attending a small liberal arts college, she drifted from one job to another in search of something she enjoyed.

When she came to see me, Naomi was working in a custom frame shop that paid minimum wage and offered no prospects for the future. She was bored, and felt adrift and clueless about what she was interested in pursuing. Over time, Naomi came to understand how she had grown up terribly confused by her family's messages about what constituted success. The educational path she had chosen, mostly by default, had snuffed out the creative desires that had motivated and gratified her in the past. Through therapy, she was able to reconnect with those parts of herself and take the first tentative steps toward finding her way.

THE RIGHT KIND OF PRESSURE

Knowing that this generation of girls is already feeling terribly pressured to achieve, how can mothers and fathers support them without adding to their stress? When does loving encouragement become intrusive or demanding? Here the parenting waters get really murky. What works well for one daughter might fail miserably with another. And what may be the right way to help your daughter succeed now may be entirely wrong later. The key to figuring out your parental approach is gauging your daughter's stress level and sensing what she needs from you at any given moment.

For example, if she is generally motivated and responsible, she may require (and desire) little input from you. Even after getting a bad grade, if she adjusts her study routine or changes tacks on her own, your involvement in that process could be counterproductive, more apt to heighten than to relieve her stress. If, however, your daughter is in crisis or on the verge of one, of course you will have to step in. The chapters that follow describe how to do so most effectively for each of the five profiles of at-risk girls.

Listening to teens, though, we can get valuable pointers on what we can do in general to reduce our daughters' stress. Time and again I hear girls distinguish between parents who are helpful and those who are "annoying." Parents in the first category (1) adopt an empathic, uncritical stance that makes girls feel supported; (2) free girls to discover and pursue their own passions rather than requiring them to live out parental dreams; (3) form broad and flexible expectations for success; and (4) make their number-one priority developing and maintaining good relationships with their daughters.

An Empathic, Uncritical Stance

Many parents who believe they are "just trying to help" tell me they are baffled because their teen daughters "flip out every time I say a word." The explanation is this: Whether our daughters see us as helpful or harmful depends not so much on what we say as on the emotions behind our words. Girls sense our empathy—or lack thereof—instantly. What determines their reaction is whether they believe we are on their side.

Two high school students, Parvin and Leah, have immigrant parents who strongly value achievement, yet the girls react far differently to their mothers' advice. Parvin, who is a highly functioning student in an independent school, told me:

> *I'm a first-generation American. My parents didn't go to college here, they went in Iran, and so they don't know that much about the college system. My mom is always telling me that she doesn't get anywhere at her work because of her speaking skills. She doesn't get promotions. She tells me, "You'll have the problem I have if you don't work harder."*

Parvin channels her mother's admonitions into a strong drive to succeed. As she said, "Everyone around you is very dedicated. You need to fulfill your parents' expectations. They sent you here to get a higher education, not to slack off."

Like many resilient girls, Parvin is better able to manage achievement-related stress because she sees her parents as loving and supportive. She thinks they genuinely care about her future and believe she can succeed. More important, Parvin knows in her heart of hearts that her mother wants her to achieve so that her life will be easier. She wants Parvin to succeed not to make up for her own difficulties, but for Parvin. That is why she is able to hear, benefit from, and even take comfort from her mother's words.

In contrast, Leah finds her mother, a first-generation Asian woman, a source of tremendous pressure. "She wants me to be happy and have enough wealth to live comfortably. She wants me to go to a good college and have a good career so I can have more than she can give me now." Although these words are similar to what Parvin hears, Leah detects a critical undercurrent. "No matter what grade you're getting, you always have to be studying. And besides doing good in all your classes, you have to be well rounded extracurricularly." Whatever Leah does, she never feels as if it is enough for her mother. Worse, she believes she can never *be* enough for her mother.

Freedom to Discover Their Passions

Because this generation of parents is savvier, more attentive, and far more involved, a new kind of relationship has evolved between teens and their mothers and fathers. Yet this closeness often engenders overinvolvement. One educator I spoke with described this shift over the course of her thirty-five-year career: "In my generation, kids were seen and not heard; we had our own lives to lead. Now girls are closer to their parents but don't have a life of their own. They're seen as their parents' productions in every sense of the word."

To want great things for our kids is perfectly normal. But to need our girls to achieve for *us* burdens them far too much. Do you look at your daughter's success as a measure of your own abilities— for example, your skills in raising her? As the vice principal of a large, regional high school told me, "Parents would say that they don't really care what their kids' grades are, but in most cases they do. They're all trying to do the right thing. But a lot of parents get the idea that they're measured by how their children are doing and by what their children are looking like."

If girls sense that their mothers or fathers are counting on their achievements to feel gratified and more confident as parents, nervous energy can hit the red zone. On the one hand, teens who excel know they are giving their parents vicarious kudos for producing an extraordinary child. This is a heady experience for any young person. But on the other hand, many stressed-out girls already find it hard to handle mistakes or defeat. What if they believe they have failed their parents as well? The stress of succeeding for everyone is too much for girls to bear.

Only children are particularly likely to take on this untenable pressure: At the end of a focus group Adrienne comments, "It's worse if you're an only child."

"Yeah," agrees her friend, who is also an only child. "All their hopes are through you. They're living vicariously through you."

Adrienne replies, "They have nothing to compare you to either."

At this point another girl at the table smiles enigmatically. "Oh yes, they do . . . ," she says. The rest of us wait as she pauses. "To themselves."

If you are completely honest with yourself, can you say that your dreams for your daughter are based primarily on her strengths and interests? Or do your goals for her result from not fulfilling your own? Might you need your daughter to succeed in order to satisfy your competitive urges, such as with your own siblings or colleagues? If so, don't berate yourself. But realize that until you modify these expectations, you are placing your daughter at a distinct disadvantage to cope with stress. As Amanda astutely says, "Pressure isn't necessarily a bad thing. It makes you more stressed, but you need it. It's only bad when everything, every success, is no longer for you—but for your parents."

Broad and Flexible Expectations

When parents predetermine and paint overly detailed pictures of what their daughters' futures should look like, trouble usually brews. The narrower parents' conception of success, the greater the pressure—for everyone in the family. Even young girls get this. As Gretchen writes in an e-mail:

> *I am about ready to blow, I am so stressed out with all my schoolwork. I barely ever have time to kick back and relax and have fun. My dad is constantly telling me that I should become*

a doctor and go to some big good school so I can live the easy
life. I don't want people to tell me what to be. I want to be a
dentist. I still have plenty of time to figure it out too. I'm a kid.

Gretchen is all of eleven.

If you convey to your daughter that she has to make a certain team, achieve a certain social status, or attend a specific college (such as the one you graduated from), you are probably going to provoke a similar reaction. Don't assume your daughter couldn't possibly have come to such a conclusion. You may be surprised. If she sees that family members achieve in particular ways, she may think, "If everyone else did it, I have to as well." Girls are anxious to maintain family standards.

Kamiko tells the group, "A lot of kids are achievers in our family. We don't do dance or sports. We're set on academics." She said this as if it were carved in stone. That is just the way it is. "My sister got into Harvard," she continues. "She got 1600 on her SATs." Whether family members are talented students, musicians, athletes, or artists, girls suffer when they think they can't be different; that is when they feel out of place, like square pegs that don't fit in.

To avoid failure, stressed-out teens often decide prematurely that they can't compete. One of the quietest girls in a focus group suddenly spoke up about this. "I'm adopted," Germaine announced. "My sisters are all beautiful and they're so good at everything. I stopped basketball. It was too much pressure, and I didn't enjoy it anymore. It drives you insane." At least Germaine knew herself and was courageous enough to quit. But her self-deprecation came through loudly and clearly.

Another problem with narrow family expectations is that they hamper girls' developmental efforts to figure out who they are. Tara, a high school junior, says she feels angry and discouraged "each time my parents see my report card and tell me, 'You could be doing better.' But what does that mean? This is how I always do," she protests. "I try my best, but they never think I do." Not only does she feel blamed for not meeting the high standards they hint at, but also she is confused about why her parents seem to see potential in her that she doesn't see. Their reaction makes her think they don't really know her or understand her.

Perhaps the most detrimental effect of teen girls' working hard to achieve their parents' goals is that they don't get to develop their own. They lose touch with their inner lives and therefore with what really gratifies them. Thea, a high school freshman, says, "When I told my parents I was going to be the salutatorian of my old [middle] school, they said, 'What happened that you're not valedictorian? You did okay, but you could've done better.' It made me look at grades just to satisfy them and not to be content with myself."

When girls' successes seem empty, they feel increasingly disengaged from their real ambitions and inclinations. Worse, they feel misunderstood, sad, discouraged, and inauthentic. Nothing good comes of this. Girls' fundamental sense of self is damaged. As one of the educators I spoke with expresses so articulately, girls in this unfortunate situation "never get to ask the critical question, 'Who am I, really?'"

Good Parent-Teen Relationships

Regardless of how successful your daughter is or which college she eventually attends, what ought to count most is the quality of your relationship. No matter what, you want to develop and maintain a close, loving connection to her that will survive long after decisions are made about her high school course schedule, which SAT IIs she takes, and what activities she continues or quits.

Along with the other, more obvious benefits of staying close, good relationships with parents seem to foster kids' success. For one, girls who see their parents' efforts as benign or helpful are more apt to internalize their values. Although about half of girls responding to my survey reported that they "always" felt pressured by their parents and teachers, far more—two thirds to three fourths—said they put this extreme level of pressure on themselves. (Incidentally, girls are 17 percent more likely than boys to pressure themselves to get good grades and do well in school.)

Teens who get along with their parents are also more motivated to achieve; they want to maintain the confidence and good will in their relationships. As Anna told me, "My mom doesn't pressure me into doing well. I just do it automatically to make her happy. It's easier on our relationship when we're both happy. Our relationship motivates me." Similarly, Talia said, "What motivates me is my dad and my mom. If they know I'm getting good grades, they'll let me go out more. If I say I'll get to my work, I want them to be able to trust me so they'll know I'm mature and can do other things."

When teens feel that achievement is pushed down their throats, or they experience their parents constantly harping on them, they are apt to become embroiled in power struggles. Eager to assert their autonomy, they regain control by doing exactly the opposite of what their parents want—that is, they perform *more* poorly. Their underachievement essentially says to their parents, "You can't make me!"

Judith, a spunky junior in a competitive high school, tells our focus group how her own motivation to go the extra step returned as soon as her mother let up on what had felt like unbearable pressure:

> *Last year my mom kept pushing me to be taking lessons, to be in the school play, and the more she pushed me, the more I wanted her to stop. I'm not rebellious. I get along really well. But she kept drilling it into me; it got to be this big stress, and*

*it made me want to stop even though I love theater. Then she
started to back off and let me find what I wanted to do and
where I wanted to do it. I looked into things over the summer
and did it. I had her support the whole time.*

Now that you are more aware of the dynamics that contribute
to girls' stress, you will be prepared to explore with your daughter
the assumptions she may be making about your expectations and
her status within the family. You will also be sensitive to the possibility that she is hiding her most painful thoughts about how she
measures up—or doesn't. You now have the opportunity to step in
and set her straight or make adjustments that reduce competitive
feelings. Above all, if you examine your own reactions and decide
you are getting caught up in heightened nervous energy, you can
always pull back a notch or two.

You cannot eliminate your daughter's pressures around success.
All of our girls struggle at times. But whether your daughter seems
to be sailing through, is showing signs of struggle, or is in the
throes of a crisis, the next part of this book will help you to identify her vulnerabilities to stress. Learning about other girls will
help you to better understand your own daughter's baffling or
seemingly self-defeating behavior and also to translate her less
than revealing words. Seeing your teen through the sharpened lens
of these new insights, you will be far better able to decide if, when,
and how to get involved in encouraging her success.

PART TWO

VULNERABILITIES TO STRESS

CHAPTER 4

Challenged by Transitions: Adapting Girls

Beginning middle school or high school—or transferring to another school—may be a rite of passage, but it is a classic trigger for girls' nervous energy. Taking the next step can seem daunting. Teens have to adjust to entirely new surroundings and educational routines, different teachers, new classmates, and usually more rigorous academic demands. Most girls face these normal, even routine, challenges (albeit on a smaller scale) at the start of every school year. Yet it is important to remember that adapting to change is inherently stressful. It is especially so for adolescent girls who are sensitive to whether they are measuring up to everyone's expectations.

Girls who are chronically insecure about peer acceptance, for example, are stressed by the prospect of trying to find their niche among a new and possibly larger set of classmates. Teens who have felt like square pegs in their families or previous schools are in a similar situation, anxious to see if they will fit in better. Perfectionistic girls are hard pressed to prove themselves all over again, and transitions add further cumulative stress to teens who are already distracted by personal problems.

During transitions the most vulnerable girls may be those who always have a hard time dealing with change. As young girls, they take their time to warm up to new people or novel experiences and are thrown off when their bus routes change or their teachers leave midyear. As they get older, they become worried and self-conscious when they go to camp for the first time, join youth groups, or start new sports. If this is your daughter's pattern, you will probably be more mindful of easing her anxiety during the first days or weeks of middle school or high school.

Yet, ironically, some girls actually do better as a result of these early struggles. They cope with stressful transitions by reminding themselves of what helped them in the past. For example, resilient teens know that they usually feel okay after the first month, when they figure out what their new teachers want. Others realize they will be fine once they find someone to sit with in each class and, especially, at lunch. Still others know that doing well on their first tests or papers will assure them and help them relax.

Many times, however, teens are caught by surprise when they have trouble. These girls are often excited about their new schools. They look forward to more freedom and better social opportunities. Then they are disconcerted when they hit obstacles—academic or social—that they never anticipated. Some of these teens do not even associate their difficulties with starting middle school or high school.

Neither do many of their parents. And yet transitions can be just as stressful for mothers and fathers. More than for parents of other at-risk girls, perhaps, these parents often see abrupt changes in their daughters—and the sudden onset of difficulties. When girls become inundated by assignments or their grades take a nosedive, parents can become alarmed about possible learning problems. This is the reason I am asked to see so many sixth and ninth graders for psychoeducational testing. Later in this chapter you will find guidelines to help you decide whether your daughter needs further evaluation and if so, how that testing should be performed.

Parents also have to adjust to a myriad of changes in their daughters' and, consequently, in their own lives. For some families, an oldest child's entry into the next level of school is nothing short of culture shock. Suddenly mothers and fathers have to deal with untried social situations such as concerts, coed parties, proms, or sleepovers, often involving new friends and friends' parents they may not even know. These are rites of passage for which few parents feel emotionally prepared.

These are some of the reasons why the beginnings of middle school and high school are high-risk times, sometimes triggering crises that can leave families feeling confused, frustrated, embattled, and most often worried about what to do. The stories filling this chapter illustrate the challenges hidden beneath teen girls' most typical behaviors, the toll of their stress, and the solutions parents often use—more or less successfully—to help them through transitions.

HOLLY

A Rocky Start

Three months into sixth grade, Marjorie calls my office in a panic to ask if I will see her daughter, Holly, who is an only child. She and her husband fear they are in a crisis—or headed for one. Not only is Holly doing poorly in school, but she also seems completely unconcerned about it. This is a drastic change from elementary school, when she was an excellent, highly motivated student. Back then Marjorie and her husband set aside their own nightly paperwork to help Holly with her homework. When her mother sat down with her to review information and quiz her, Holly's confidence soared along with her grades.

But since middle school, and despite her slipping grades, Holly has begun to chafe against her parents' involvement in her work. Dreading the inevitable tension, she gets off the school bus every afternoon with a chip on her shoulder. Sullen and remote, she is determined to avoid her mother's questions about her day. And when Marjorie tries to stay on top of Holly's assignments by asking her what she has to do, she finds that her daughter instantly erupts into anger and defiance.

But because they are so worried, Holly's parents persist. They require her to do her homework as soon as she gets home, keep track of all her due dates, and try to quiz her before her tests. Holly adamantly refuses. At first she doesn't say so, at least not in words. Instead, she passively resists by "forgetting" her assignments, dawdling, and doing the absolute minimum to get by. "You're so annoying! All you do is nag me!" Holly protests. "I'm in sixth grade! If I want your help, I'll ask for it." This sentiment is expressed by many young teens, for whom autonomy becomes precious.

When nagging backfires, Holly's mother reluctantly agrees to let up. For perhaps a week or two, Marjorie bites her tongue and restrains herself from checking on whether Holly's homework is done—or done correctly. Soon, however, several interim notices arrive in the mail reporting missing assignments and inconsistent effort; her teachers suggest extra help. Holly all but invites her mother to resume monitoring and supervising her work. Marjorie feels vindicated—yet also increasingly desperate.

She and her husband begin to blame their daughter's poor performance on the new flurry of social activity they see in middle school. It galls them that "all Holly seems to care about is her friends." While she is supposedly doing her work, her mother hears the chimes of instant messages on her computer or Holly talking excitedly on the phone. So to get their daughter to do better, they try taking away her privileges: Phone time is restricted to a half hour, and there is no more Internet. Holly is furious. "Like punishing me is really gonna help!" she yells. "It's just going to make me madder and hate you more!"

Holly is angry about how her parents are reacting and so determined to get them off her back that she begins to lie about whether she has homework or has finished it. This alarms her parents, provoking them to have long, impassioned talks with her about integrity and responsibility. When they notice that Holly makes it a point to look either annoyed or bored, they are mystified and hurt by her hostility. Overnight it seems everything is falling apart.

Holly's rocky start to middle school sets her parents scrambling to set things right. They go from confused and frustrated to distraught and helpless. Nothing they try seems to work. They are convinced that if she will just do the few things they suggest, she could catch up on her work, get better grades, and feel good about herself. But Holly makes no effort to improve. If anything, in fact, they suspect she is deliberately digging in her heels and sabotaging her own success—just to spite them.

Holly's behavior sends them mixed messages; she wants autonomy, but seems to need their involvement. This push-pull dynamic underlies many of the difficulties with transitions. As with many families tackling the challenges of middle school, cracks form in the partnership that once worked so well. Locked into a rather classic battle of wills, Holly and her parents see each other as adversaries. Upon a friend's recommendation, they bring their daughter for therapy. They do not know what else to do.

It is a raw and blustery November afternoon when Holly first comes to my office. She is wearing formfitting jeans, no jacket, and a long-sleeved T-shirt that leaves two inches of midriff exposed. Her long blond hair is pulled up in a ponytail, a white stretch headband securing stray wisps. She wears no jewelry or makeup. With her relaxed, personable manner, Holly has the demeanor of a confident sixth grader.

Like so many young teens, Holly withholds from her parents what she is thinking and feeling. In the therapy office, it becomes clear that she is equally upset about the rising tension in her family. Without preamble, her eyes dark and intense, Holly tells me:

> *As soon as I get home from school, my mother starts in on me. It's all she cares about anymore. She's always going, "Let me check your work. This answer could be better. Did you make those note cards I suggested yet? Let me see your thesis statement for your English paper; it's due Friday." She's always on my case. Can't I just go to my room and chill for a while? For God's sake, I'm not in third grade anymore!*

After complaining about her parents, Holly can admit how stressful she is finding middle school. "I'm usually good in school, but this year I'm finding sixth grade to be a lot harder," she says. "There's tons and tons of homework, and with all the other clubs and activities kids have these days, it is almost impossible to get all your work done and study for tests. My parents always pressure me to do well, but I don't know how I can get all A's and B's. I thought I'd love middle school, but I don't know."

The Hidden Challenges

Holly is far from unusual. Not all girls are ready to be more organized, to learn foreign languages, to study for midterms and finals, and to take standardized tests. Many take two steps backward for every step forward. Educators used to think that puberty was responsible for the widely observed downturn in test scores, performance, and behavior during these years. Now, blaming transition, they are recommending that K-through-8 schools replace middle schools to offer more continuity. Meanwhile, girls like Holly have rather common and predictable worries:

"Can I Make It Here?" Academically, girls facing transitions— even to the next grade—are most often apprehensive about three things: (1) having to do more work, (2) having to do different kinds of work, and (3) having to do their work more independently. Though she hasn't told her parents or teachers, Holly has worried from day one of sixth grade that she can't handle the workload. "I don't think I can even do it all," she confides. "Middle school is a big step up. The homework is just so advanced that nobody can understand it. And when they ask, the teachers get so mad and don't explain it."

Girls who are not well organized feel more pressured by having to keep track of class schedules, teachers, homework assignments, and multiple due dates all at once. Looking at her assignment book, Holly tells me, doesn't help. "I know I have a big unit test in social studies next week, but I can't really start studying because I have a take-home test in math due Friday, I have to turn in my art project on Monday, and over the weekend I have to get together with my science group to work on our project. There's so much information to remember, so many dates in social studies . . ." With that, she sighs and drops her head dramatically.

Parents often underestimate the anxiety that is also aroused by the culture of middle school, including the new regimen of rules— and the consequences for breaking them. Girls often tell me that they are afraid of getting detention for minor crimes such as talking in the hallway, getting to class late, or losing their locker combination. Holly says, "I don't know if I can get to Spanish fast enough. It's all the way on the other side of the school, and sometimes the hallway is crowded. My parents will kill me if I get a detention. Sometimes I worry, what if I accidentally break one of those billion stupid rules?"

"Will People Like Me?" Since relationships are all important to young teen girls, transitions provoke worries about how they will get along with everyone. Will they like their new teachers? Will their teachers like them, help them, and be on their side? Anxious to get off to a good start, Holly fears irritating her teachers. "It's not that they're mean or anything," she explains. "But they act all serious. And if somebody asks a question, they act like maybe they weren't paying attention or it was their fault." When she witnesses such interactions, Holly says, "I don't want to be them. I'd rather act like I get it." Thus she starts middle school too timid to speak up and determined to hide her confusion.

A new set of social rules also marks the entry to middle school. While some girls are adept at picking up on cues, making new friends, and navigating shifting cliques, others feel adrift without the anchor of reassuring connections. Many girls describe their worst school experiences as "when I didn't know anyone in my classes," "when I was lonely," and "when I didn't know anybody and felt out of place." When their trouble developing close, satisfying friendships becomes chronic and preoccupying, they may resemble the girls described in Chapter 6 who are desperate for acceptance.

But even girls who have friends in middle school grapple with dilemmas such as whether it is cool to be smart and whether their peers (especially boys) will find their strengths attractive. Girls often have to reconcile the desire to do well academically with the need to be accepted socially. For some young teens, this proves overwhelming.

Recently I saw the parents of another sixth grader who were frightened that they were losing control. Not only was their daughter, Tracy, gravitating to the most precocious girls, but she had also begun to adopt various undesirable behaviors. She was insisting on designer jeans, wearing full makeup to school, and spending hours online with her friends. Perhaps more troubling, she became angry and defiant whenever her mother said no. As Tracy tested the limits in every direction, her parents felt as if they were always several steps behind, breathlessly trying to keep up with her. Temporarily, the dynamics of the family were shaken. Tracy's parents had to become proactive, reestablishing the structure and limits that made sense for their family.

Like many girls who question their academic abilities, Holly finds her social life far more satisfying than her schoolwork. It is no wonder: She is more successful with her peers. Holly may not know the European capitals, but she prides herself on rattling off the sixth grade social dos and don'ts with authority, knowing what is going on with all her friends, and helping them with their problems. Becoming something of an adviser to her peers enables Holly to retain her self-esteem in middle school. This is exactly why many middle school girls seem so desperate to be in touch with their friends—and react so vehemently when their parents restrict their social lives.

HELPING GIRLS IN TRANSITION

It is hard for parents to watch powerlessly while girls fall behind in their work, get poor grades, and perhaps seem unconcerned. If your daughter doesn't do well this year, you may worry about how her performance will affect her placement next year, such as whether she is recommended to take honors classes or stay in an accelerated track. Like many parents with daughters in this age group, you may be upset about clashing more with your daughter and perplexed about why your perfectly reasonable solutions are rejected. You have yet to find the secret code that will unlock your daughter's motivation and cooperation. If so, these suggestions may help:

▶ Re-create Positive Alliances

First re-create a strong alliance with your daughter. To reverse the climate of negativity, it is necessary to reduce emotional intensity, worry, and blame. Speaking with teachers or counselors about adolescent development can alleviate anxiety and confusion about what is typical. Holly's parents are reassured to learn that girls entering middle school often go through an adjustment period. They are also calmed by the fact that developing new social ties is a valid and important task of early adolescence. This helps them to keep their own trepidation from spilling over into their interactions with Holly.

Parents also have to take the lead in defusing power struggles. Pay close attention to your initial conversations after school. Nearly every mother and father tells of asking innocuous questions such as "How was your day?" or "How hard was your math test?" and then feeling mystified and helpless when horrific arguments erupt. How could their heartfelt interest and good intentions be so misconstrued?

As Marjorie tells it, her daughter goes berserk the moment she walks in the door. As Holly sees it, her mother jumps on her and interrogates her before she has a chance to unwind from her stressful school day. This classic scenario can be avoided if parents are mindful of their daughters' cues. When can girls best tolerate such discussions? At bedtime? While running errands? Right after school is rarely the ideal time.

Parents also must examine their emotional tone. Although Marjorie believes her questions are casual, Holly finds them intrusive and anxiety provoking because she senses accusatory undercurrents. This is hardly surprising. Teen girls already feel scrutinized, so they are hypersensitive to being probed. Holly explains, "It's one thing to ask what I learned today or if anything interesting happened; it's another to get into this test grade, or what my teacher said about my project, or what the class average was. I can't take it when she butts in!"

What Holly is really saying is that these sorts of focused questions convey all too clearly her parents' anxiety, which intensifies her own nervous energy—and sometimes provokes her less controlled responses. Feeling overwhelmed by their parents' angst, girls tend to snap, become rude or sarcastic, and stomp off to their rooms. They are also more compelled to keep their own worries—and mistakes—well hidden. As Holly explains, "Why would I want my parents to know when I screw up? Why do they need to know how stressed I am? If they get more freaked, then what? They'd just nag me more about my homework or make sure I'm not 'wasting time' online. That's all I need!"

Marjorie becomes less resentful and defensive when she understands that deep down Holly fears messing up and, therefore, disappointing and upsetting her. Especially when her mother helps her with her homework, Holly feels as if a poor grade fails both of them. She is afraid that her mistakes will eventually alienate her mother, as if one more C will make her mother give up on her: "I didn't do that well on a notebook quiz the other day. All I could think about was what my mother was going to say. She'd be thinking how hopeless I am. Maybe she won't even help me anymore."

Attributing her own self-recriminations to her mother, Holly expects her mother to treat her like a lost cause—and then reacts to her mother's innocuous comments as if she already is. To defuse such perceptions, parents can focus less on their daughters' mistakes and more on what they are doing right. This is not easy to do, particularly when there are difficulties and anxiety is running high. But Holly, like most teen girls, responds better to praise than to criticism. Feeling valued by her parents is part of the secret code that unlocks her motivation and offers the possibility of improvement.

▶ Provide Appropriate Support

The question of how much help is helpful—and appropriate—is a tricky issue for many parents. Some girls want their mothers or fathers to be virtual collaborators on all their assignments. Others prefer a hands-off policy. In deciding what makes sense, parents are wise to consider their daughter's preferences in the context of her age and academic needs. Transitions often signal a need for parents to change as well, offering progressively less help as girls mature. If in doubt, ask her teachers how much parental input they expect. In general, offer only as much help as daughters need. When this works well, I hear something on the order of, "I like it when my parents ask me if I need help. If I do, they help me. If I don't, they back off."

It is especially difficult to maintain an ideal level of involvement when daughters are struggling academically. In fact, this is when parents tend to panic and cross the line. For this reason, Marjorie's help becomes toxic. "She thinks she's helping me," complains Holly, "but she's not. She's just confusing me more." When Holly's grades don't improve, Marjorie takes these accusations to heart, asking what she could have done wrong and trying ever harder to be helpful. Without intervention, this cycle continues unchecked, ratcheting up both the anxiety and the conflict in this family.

Through counseling, however, Holly's parents realize that her entry into adolescence requires them to create a more collaborative relationship with her. Being seen as too strict or unreasonable backfires; instead, they find that prudence and flexibility go a long way. Even parents who have set the stage for good work habits early on, such as by setting limits for television and computer games during the week, find that as daughters mature and their needs change, the rules about such privileges have to be renegotiated, often over and again.

Rather than dictating a new study plan, Holly's parents ask her what she thinks will help her get her work done. They eventually agree on a schedule that includes a balance of study hours, activities, and downtime. With new appreciation and respect for Holly's need to socialize, they are careful to carve out time for her friends. Like many parents of middle school students who are exuberant about new extracurricular opportunities, they also have to insist that she not take on too much at once.

Holly is grateful to her parents for finding a tutor to help her improve her study skills. Working with a neutral individual defuses the emotional intensity of her mother's involvement. Holly's parents also tell her that this arrangement is a work in progress, and that they are open to considering changes whenever the need arises.

Although many anxious parents become overly involved in school, others do not get involved enough. Thinking their input is neither needed nor desired, or to avoid the resurgence of their old feelings about achievement, they keep their distance and give their daughters free rein. Yet less disciplined teens often run amok, especially during transitions. Without structure and supervision, they can't manage. Schoolwork and other responsibilities are neglected until parents or teachers are forced to step in.

It is better to be proactive in determining the degree of involvement that is right for your daughter. These suggestions, based on my experiences with all girls in middle school and high school, may help to differentiate between helpful versus intrusive parental support with homework:

+ Give girls their own study spaces and stock them with all needed school supplies to avoid last-minute scrambling for pencils or paper clips.

+ To facilitate organization, abide by the motto "A place for everything, and everything in its place." This enables everyone in the family to know exactly where to find the thesaurus, calculator, and hole punch.

+ Help girls get started. Review the instructions and grading rubric, if provided. Brainstorm a plan. Anticipate obstacles and how to circumvent them. This relieves anxiety and gives girls momentum.

+ If they're lonely and ask for company, curl up with a good book while they work.

+ Don't make decisions for them, such as their term paper topic, or give them all the reasons why their choices are wrong.

+ If they ask a question, answer it briefly and then let them get back to work. If they expect to hear a long lecture, they'll hesitate to ask you in the future.

+ Don't hover; it makes them nervous.

+ In a pinch, be willing to pitch in with time-consuming but mindless tasks such as gluing or covering textbooks.

+ Be careful of contradicting their teachers, which confuses them.

+ Limit your help to what is requested; for example, don't check grammar or spelling unless they ask you to, and if you are asked to edit a paper, don't rewrite it.

+ Be available for last-minute runs to the library or office supply store.

+ If girls don't finish their work, don't rescue them by writing excuses to their teachers; let them experience and learn from the consequences.

+ Convey your interest and excitement about what they are learning.

+ Join a parent support group in your community. Or start one.

► Use the School as a Resource

It is often unclear when to ask the school for help—and how best to do so. When teens take that next step into middle school or high school, we usually have less contact with our daughters' teachers and don't feel as included in the educational process. Many parents are reluctant to divulge their concerns for fear of biasing teachers against their daughters. Also, some hesitate to approach schools because as teenagers they felt powerless, ignored, misunderstood, or intimidated by their own teachers or administrators.

Schools are generally receptive to questions and concerns about students' progress. When you contact the designated individual—a team leader, guidance counselor, head teacher, middle school or high school director, or head of school—he or she will survey your daughter's teachers about the information you request, such as test grades, general behavior, or homework compliance, and get back to you. Depending on how much girls are struggling, this can be done on a weekly or biweekly basis. Feedback from schools can also give students and parents input about whether tutoring, study skills training, or other sorts of outside help are needed. Best of all, parent-teen relationships benefit because mothers and fathers no longer have to police girls.

When girls are struggling, it is easy for everyone involved to point fingers or become defensive. During transitions, it is especially confusing to sort out everyone's changing roles. Teens have the best chance of thriving, however, when their parents and teachers maintain a cordial, constructive relationship. Whether girls are in middle school or high school, these guidelines may be helpful in approaching and collaborating productively with teachers, guidance counselors, and administrators:

◆ Develop the mind-set that educational personnel are valuable resources for getting information about students and their school experiences, including their progress in courses, test performance, attitude, effort, and classroom behavior.

◆ Attend the school's open house at the beginning of the year to meet teachers and hear about their syllabi, expectations, grading policies, and so forth.

◆ Think of teachers as partners whose common goals are ensuring that students function as well as possible and make the best use of their education.

◆ Recognize that because school personnel have seen hundreds of girls during their careers, they can offer a valuable perspective on where individual girls stand in relation to their peers.

◆ To convey respect for the teacher's professional time, call ahead to schedule a meeting rather than stopping in without warning. Be respectful by showing up on time and not prolonging the meeting.

◆ Rather than coming across as accusatory by giving your daughter's side of a conflict, try "My daughter is very upset. Help me to understand the situation." If the teacher has done something inappropriate, it will come out in the process.

◆ Be open to hearing teachers' negative feedback without becoming defensive, dismissing their observations, or attempting to disprove them.

◆ In turn, be honest about a student's weaknesses as well as her strengths and how she typically reacts to change, handles academic challenges, and deals with classroom situations.

◆ Try to ignore the opinions of other parents, rumors about any teacher's alleged flaws, or even previous disappointing experiences. Treat each meeting with school personnel as a fresh start.

✦ If there is a need for ongoing communication, arrange with each teacher how often and by what modality it should take place (for example, weekly, via e-mail, by phone, scheduled conferences, notes in the backpack, and so on). Many teachers rely on e-mail as an easy conduit for frequent correspondence to track kids' progress.

✦ When girls have problems with specific teachers, it is usually best to address them directly with those individuals rather than go above their heads to department heads, guidance counselors, or administrators (see Chapter 10).

✦ After meetings with schools, it is important to give girls honest, age-appropriate feedback about what their teachers have shared about them.

VALERY

Bigger Kids, Bigger Problems

You might think that adjusting to middle school has prepared your daughter for high school. But in addition to reexperiencing many of the previous challenges, girls starting high school face different and even greater developmental hurdles. Many struggles remain invisible to parents, yet just as easily wreak havoc on girls' adjustment and cause disturbances at home. Whether your daughter is adapting to high school right now or preparing to do so in the future, you may find Valery's experiences informative.

After participating in my ongoing freshman focus group, Valery is eager to be interviewed individually; she clearly has a need to talk more about what she is going through this year. She says she finds this large, diverse regional high school a breath of fresh air after the "narrow-mindedness" of her much smaller, local middle school. At the same time, it is harder than she had imagined. As we make our way around her study hall, which is held in a large cafeteria, she glances furtively around the room and walks with a tense posture. Clearly, Valery is not all that comfortable or relaxed. Being a new student again has caused a resurgence of her former self-consciousness.

The transition to high school often serves as a marker, causing teens to pause and take stock of where they stand in the self-discovery process that is central to middle adolescence. With their thinking abilities developing throughout adolescence, girls are increasingly able to grasp concepts, analyze, and plan. They are more aware of weighing academic choices, setting goals, and figuring out who they are. Freshman year is all about imagining the possibilities and recognizing the challenges that lie ahead. Valery describes it this way:

> Grades just came out and spring sports are starting up, and I was thinking how successful do I want to be in all those areas and what does it mean. I'm finding myself and finding what kind of successes I want. I'm very comfortable in school with my friends and I've met a lot of new people. It's been a great experience, but I don't think I'm even close to figuring all I can be yet. It's hard being a freshman.

Academics are foremost on Valery's mind. "I really slacked off in eighth grade," she tells me. "My laziness drove my parents crazy. They got me a tutor." Valery is one of two daughters of a dual-career couple. Her father is a banker, her mother the vice president of a public relations firm. In this family, a good education is the top priority. Valery says, "I guess I do want to do better this year. I have to get serious now. High school is a chance to start over. This counts." She is alluding to the fact that college admissions officers will see her freshman grades on her high school transcript. From day one of high school, this realization haunts her and heightens her daily pressure.

Hitting a Wall

Much to her chagrin, Valery's newfound motivation doesn't translate into better grades. Like many high school freshmen, she has trouble setting priorities and managing her time. Valery hasn't studied as thoroughly as she knows she should have for a big test. "Deep down, I knew I had to memorize a lot of notes, and I could have done it. But I thought I would be fine if I just read them. I thought I could get away with it," she admits. "I guess I just wasn't into spending all that time. Lots of my friends were having birthdays and get-togethers. I wanted to have a good balance."

Valery is terribly upset when she gets back her midterms. "We all heard about these exams, and we got so stressed out about it. We didn't really know how to study for them, so we all failed," she laments. "I got two A's, and then I went down to two C's and a D." Like many freshmen, even when Valery thinks she studied enough and knows the material inside out, her grades don't always reflect what she believes she knows.

This is when girls learn that their study skills are no longer working for them and they are forced to stretch. "Where did I go wrong?" Valery asks wistfully. "We discussed my grade, me and my English teacher. She's missing three of my assignments. That's what hurt me. I also made mistakes. I didn't use any textual support." Valery reiterates this point, as if underscoring its importance. "If you want to do well, you have to use more textual support than you did in eighth grade."

It is obvious that she is trying to come to terms with this setback. "It's bad because you know you can do better. It's frustrating.

You have to do better. It kind of freaked me out, but I got over it. I try not to beat myself up too much." But like all girls, her sense of failure is heightened when she thinks about how her parents will react. And so she keeps them completely in the dark about her distress.

A Family's Response

Valery believes that because of her lackluster performance in eighth grade, her parents have been watching her closely in high school. When her grades drop further, they tell her that she must not be trying hard enough, and they explain how important it is for her to do well. This is not the response she wants or needs. As Valery sees it, they "lecture" her nonstop, making her feel not only criticized but also rejected. She thinks her parents want her to be someone else entirely:

> My parents are totally on my case this year. When they see my grades, they flip out. My father tells me I should be studying more. He wants me to read more, like for pleasure. They think I'm capable of doing so much better than I am. I guess that's true. But they think I should be just like their friends' kids, getting straight A's or A pluses, doing my homework, and then reading classics just for fun. It makes me so mad when they say stuff and compare me to other people.

Hurt and angry, Valery becomes even more determined to withhold information and act indifferent to their concerns. Even when she aces her biology test and gets an A minus on an English paper, she won't give them the satisfaction of telling them. As the rupture in their relationship widens, Valery's parents are desperate to help her. But when they ground her and speak to her guidance counselor without her knowledge, she becomes incensed. "They have no right to interfere in my life," she rages. "They can't just barge in here and talk to people behind my back."

What She Keeps Hidden

When I ask Valery if she has talked to her parents about being a freshman, she looks aghast. "Of course not! That's not something I would ever tell them!" she exclaims. "I can't explain how weird it is when you hear people saying stuff about us freshman in the hallways. And a lot of senior and junior guys are in the halls, hanging around, and the teachers aren't standing there. The worst pressure comes from them, to be with them sexually. How can I tell them that?"

She takes a quick breath and continues to rant. "How could I explain how crazy mood swings are in high school? If a guy is acting all weird or you're depressed because you've had a fight, it's hard. They're not gonna understand that it's distracting when you're trying to figure out plans on the weekend. It's hard to sit down and do work on a Saturday when you're stressed out about what to do that night."

Because she is entrenched in feeling angry, misunderstood, and mistreated by her parents, Valery cannot bring herself to drop her façade of indifference and admit how worried she is about producing what her teachers now expect: "In middle school, you could do it halfway and teachers wouldn't even notice. To be a genius, all you had to do is memorize stuff. But in high school you have to earn the grades you get. You have to really understand what you're talking about. Teachers are more critical."

Without the study guides she got in middle school, she feels more unsure of herself before big tests. She says, "Midterms and finals count for a lot more and cover larger amounts of material. You can't make up a bad grade with extra credit here. And participation doesn't even count as much."

Being tracked in high school intensifies Valery's self-scrutiny by highlighting precisely where she stands in relation to her classmates. Her self-esteem, success in the classroom, and friendships are affected. "My friends are in smart classes, advanced honors classes," she confides. "I'm in normal classes. My best friend moved up to a higher level, but I stayed. We only see each other in one class now." Valery is coping with these losses and challenges, but the adjustment process has not been easy.

MAKING NECESSARY SHIFTS

Valery's intensifying struggle with her parents impedes her working through her own internal conflicts about achievement, which is a normal part of adjusting to high school. In this case, her parents' nervous energy is like background noise, distracting her and making her defensive. Valery has to examine what she needs to do differently in school in order to feel good about herself. Along with the suggestions offered earlier in this chapter, these two strategies can help teens and their families when they hit a wall:

► Get More Information

Disappointing grades and placement in lower-level classes prompt a string of self-doubts. Girls often wonder, "Am I smart enough?" or "Why aren't I as smart as my friends?" Valery worries that she has a learning disability or attention deficit disorder, and wonders whether she needs medication. When daughters have trouble, parents have similar questions. For example, is she performing at her best or is she capable of doing better? Is she doing okay socially? Does she have a problem? And what will help her improve?

Although it is natural for parents to turn to school personnel for answers, this sort of information may be hard to get, especially from understaffed and overworked public schools, unless girls are literally failing or exhibiting flagrant behavior problems. Parents often tell me that guidance counselors try to reassure them by saying that their daughter is in good company: Many students have similar issues. Although this may be true, my clinical experience tells me it is always wise to trust parents' gut instincts; when they sense something is amiss, they are usually right.

Parents are also advised to wait and see. When teens are struggling, however, this is not always the best course. Nervous energy and frustration are usually too high. And if skills need to be remedied, students lose ground. When questions remain about a girl's capabilities and weaknesses, I believe a thorough psychoeducational evaluation of her reasoning, problem solving, academic skills, and emotional functioning can provide the answers to set everyone's mind at ease.

When Is Further Evaluation Warranted?

One or more of these red flags should signal a need for further assessment:

+ School performance is markedly erratic or inexplicably deteriorating.
+ Standardized testing is poor or significantly discrepant from grades.
+ The school recommends further evaluation.
+ Girls seem to forget previous learning.

+ Specific subjects prove chronically difficult.
+ Teens suddenly begin to dislike school.
+ School papers and materials are extremely disorganized.
+ Students avoid school by staying home sick, skipping classes, or being truant.
+ Homework is unduly stressful, takes too long, or is often incomplete.
+ Girls complain of not being able to pay attention or being distractible in class.
+ Behavior in class suddenly becomes disruptive.
+ Teens say they feel different or wonder what is wrong with them.
+ There are changes in sleep habits, mood, weight loss, or other at-risk behaviors.
+ Girls ask for medication.

The best way to find a competent professional is to ask for a personal recommendation from a friend or your daughter's school or her physician—not the yellow pages. In addition, these are some issues to consider when choosing an evaluator:

Guidelines for Psychoeducational Evaluations

+ Make sure the evaluator is a psychologist or neuropsychologist trained to work with adolescents, as well as someone your daughter will feel comfortable with.
+ Ideally, testing should take place over two or more sessions so the evaluator has a chance to get to know her on more than one occasion.

+ Evaluators should obtain information from parents and teachers in addition to using their own observations and findings from tests.
+ Testing should include the assessment of the student's cognitive abilities, achievement, neuropsychological functions, such as attention and memory skills, and personality (social and emotional functioning).
+ Results should be communicated to parents promptly—and in language that is easily understood.
+ A written report should be provided.
+ The evaluation should produce specific, usable, and helpful recommendations.

Objective information gained from testing, especially when explained by a professional rather than a parent, helps girls to understand and come to terms with who they are. Teens light up when told about their strengths and generally feel relieved when they find out about specific weaknesses. Facts put their worst fears to rest. They learn that their struggles are not their fault, that they are not stupid, and that there are resources available to help them. Also, by discovering their learning styles, girls can add valuable strategies to their study repertoires and perform better.

► Empower Girls to Be Proactive

High school challenges girls to take on increasing responsibility for their success. But when parent-teen tension about achievement struggles aggravates normal adolescent secrecy, mothers and fathers may not have a clue whether their daughters are being diligent and proactive or passively waiting for something to change. If you don't know what your daughter is or is not doing, don't assume she has dropped the ball. Instead, try asking her something on the order of, "What are you trying now?" or "Have you considered asking your teacher what you can do to improve?" or "Do you need help?"

Because she is locking horns with her parents, Valery doesn't tell them about the positive outcome of her poor midterm grade. But she wondered where she went wrong, and so she took the initiative to speak with her English teacher. "I was so afraid to talk to him," Valery tells me, "but I kept telling myself what to say, in my head, and then one day after school I just went up to him and asked how he grades those papers." Armed with a clearer idea of how she can do better on the next writing assignment, Valery felt empowered.

And she came away knowing that her teacher admired her assertiveness. Valery tells me, "He said he was really impressed that I came to him directly instead of going to guidance or getting my parents to call. He said I'm off to a good start." A few minutes later Valery repeats this, almost verbatim. She is clearly proud of herself because her teacher acknowledged and rewarded her initiative. Yet unless she shares this success with her parents, they will continue to take her silence as evidence that she hasn't taken care of the problem—or worse, doesn't care about the problem.

Other girls may need encouragement to approach their teachers. If your daughter is uncomfortable, find out why so you can ease her concerns. She may have to be coached on how to express herself effectively. Role-playing often gives teens much-needed confidence in these situations. If such efforts don't pay off, the next step may be for the family to meet with the teacher and/or with the guidance counselor.

With greater insight into the sorts of misimpressions and misunderstandings that typically plague girls and their parents during times of transition, you may be better able to avoid these scenarios with your own daughter and maintain a good relationship during stressful transitions. Even when she isn't forthcoming, this knowledge may help you to read between the lines, interpret her behavior accurately, empathize, and become only as involved as necessary. That way you have the best chance of helping her to keep her life in balance and to develop both the skills and confidence she needs to succeed in her new school.

CHAPTER 5

Square Peg Dilemmas: Undervalued Girls

Teen girls feel most successful when their accomplishments are reflected in the eyes of the people who matter most to them: their parents, teachers, and peers. Those who feel fundamentally different from their families or classmates, however, may find it hard to get that affirmation. While more resilient girls might rejoice in their individuality, vulnerable girls believe their particular talents and interests are not valued. They are stressed by thinking they will never meet others' expectations, that they will never be respected or seen as one of the best. These girls think of themselves as square pegs in round holes.

All teens have moments like this. Because of circumstances or their own sensitivities, they may temporarily fear not fitting the mold. Although girls in transition usually worry about fitting in with new classmates, this anxiety abates as soon as they find their group. Insecure girls are desperate to feel accepted by their peers and teachers, and distracted girls who are preoccupied with problems often feel isolated. But unlike these other at-risk groups, square pegs perceive themselves as worlds apart from the people around them. They think of themselves as perpetual misfits.

Square pegs don't think they match up to traditional standards of success. For example, some live to act, dance, or sing, but aren't interested in school. Others love to create poetry, sculpture, or cartoons, but shy away from reading books and writing research papers. Classic scenarios for feeling undervalued include tone-deaf teens having musical siblings, klutzes attending schools that revere athletes, and artsy girls coming from scholarly families or attending academically rigorous schools.

Emily, a junior, says, "Everyone in my school is so top-notch, I just feel under that. I'm always being compared to someone who's higher than I am. I want to be an actress, but my friends ask me, 'What's your real job going to be?'" Most vulnerable are girls who are truly offbeat or quirky, who simply march to their own drummers.

With the cultural frenzy about academic achievement, parents and schools are well aware of the litany of requirements teenage girls must fulfill to be successful today. No wonder we get anxious when our kids don't look conventional. It frightens us to think their nonconformity will prevent their success later on. It is also harder to support girls who have unfamiliar interests or follow unpredictable adolescent paths. With their typical perceptiveness, even young girls detect and absorb these apprehensions.

Although Emmie is only eight, she senses her father's anxiety about her progress in school. Steve, a thoughtful Harvard-educated physicist, confesses sheepishly that although he knows better, he finds himself mildly upset when Emmie is placed in the middle reading group of her class. One evening, when Steve reminds her that she is supposed to read to a parent, she protests, "No, Daddy, not with you. I want to read to Mommy." When Steve asks her why, Emmie replies, "You care too much."

The stress of believing they can never measure up takes its toll by damaging girls' self-esteem. As Kristin, a *Girls' Life* reader, put it, "I feel like I can't do anything right sometimes and everyone else can do better than me. How can I relax with what I've got and not what I don't have?" When undervalued girls give up and stop trying to please the people who matter to them, their relationships with their parents and teachers often deteriorate.

More resilient teens, on the other hand, flourish because they can count on the adults in their lives to recognize and honor their individuality as well as to validate and nurture their talents. Yet when parents see daughters struggling, it is easy to pressure them to conform, to do better, or to make more friends. In the process, we can miss the underlying issue: a daughter who feels terribly misunderstood because her talents lie elsewhere. This is what happened with Claire, a delightful, extremely attractive teenager I saw in therapy.

CLAIRE

Skyrocketing Pressure

The summer before Claire's junior year, her mother calls my office to make an appointment for her. School has always been a struggle, she tells me, and since this will be Claire's most important year of high school, they want her to get off to a good start. Unlike her brother, who was a solid B-plus student, Claire gets mostly B's and C's, with the occasional D when she slacks off. More worrisome to her parents is that Claire seems increasingly tired, discouraged, and apathetic about school. They have always had her work with tutors. Now they hope that therapy can help her too.

Fortunately, Claire readily agrees to talk with me. The first time we meet, I am struck by how glamorous she is, even wearing athletic shorts, a tank top, and flip-flops. Her blond hair flips evenly across her tanned shoulders, one of which bears the strap of a purse all the teenage girls are dying for. Smiling politely and firmly shaking my hand, Claire introduces herself, sits down on one of my reclining chairs, and exhales deeply.

"I hate school," she says. "Not the social part. I love seeing my friends and being a cheerleader. But I hate my classes." When I ask her to explain, Claire describes feeling less competent than her peers. "My friends are all really, really smart. They're in honors and AP classes," she tells me. "The perfect people get nothing below an A. I try not to compare myself to them. I'm in regular classes, and I still hardly get A's. It's sometimes hard for me just to get B's." This makes her feel inferior, as if she doesn't fit in.

Talking of school seems to shrivel Claire. Her shoulders slump, the lively bright-eyed expression I saw only minutes before has dimmed, and her voice trails off as if she lacks the stamina to continue. Claire attends a fairly large suburban high school that is regarded as highly competitive, both academically and socially. Feeling out of her element in the classroom and inadequate among her peers, Claire is stressed out, ashamed, and frantic to find her place. Her despair and exhaustion are obvious and understandable.

When I ask her about her interests and hobbies, she instantly perks up. With obvious pride, Claire tells me about the hard work and discipline of being a cheerleader. She is candid about the social perks as well: the camaraderie of her team, the status of cheerleaders in her school, and the invitations to parties. Claire also skis, plays field hockey, and participates on the varsity tennis team. "Sports are my thing," she says. "I'd much rather be active, doing stuff, than sitting still and reading a book."

Although it is only July, Claire is already dreading her junior year. "Just thinking about school next year makes me feel sick," she says. "I know my parents are going to be on my back twenty-four/ seven. They freaked out about my end-of-year report card and what I got on the practice PSATs. I did really bad. Now my summer is going to be ruined."

Claire is referring to the SAT prep program her parents have arranged for her. "They've been telling me how, since my grades aren't great, I have to get really good SATs if I'm going to get into

BU [Boston University]." This is the school her father attended and where her brother is starting as a freshman in the fall.

Claire is at a crossroads. Though she dislikes schoolwork and questions whether it is worth giving up her summer vacation to work on her scores, she weighs her father's beliefs: "My dad thinks success is doing great in school. Other things are sort of important, like sports, but school is always number one. And that means doing really, really well—working, working, working until you get something. So you can go to a top college." Because she perceives her parents as supportive, she has internalized their values about success and wants to please them. This is why Claire reluctantly promises to go to her tutoring sessions and do whatever work she is assigned.

Beneath her dutiful compliance, however, she is feeling increasingly distressed. It is not that she hasn't felt like a square peg in her family before. In the past, though, she was able to feel good about herself anyway because she is more athletic and popular than her brother. But junior year, with its emphasis on gearing up for the SATs and applying to college, is the stressor that threatens to topple Claire into crisis. This is when she becomes convinced that she cannot possibly live up to her parents' ideals and be a credit to them. Claire's optimism and drive crumble—along with her self-confidence.

A Crisis in the Making

Despite attending weekly tutoring sessions and taking a succession of practice tests, Claire's SAT scores do not improve as everyone had hoped. She is upset, but not devastated. It is when her parents ask about her progress that she feels most discouraged and even ashamed. Whatever disappointment teens may feel about poor grades, sports losses, or being passed over for awards is magnified exponentially by how their parents react. Claire says, "With my dad, he doesn't scream or get violent. He gives you guilt. You can see it in his face and everything."

Claire's parents are increasingly frustrated by her lack of progress. Like many mothers and fathers, they have good intentions. Yet despite my coaching during our parent sessions to ease up, they can't stop themselves from trying to fix her supposed flaws. They continually remind her about her appointments, test dates, and supposed goals. They repeatedly replace her SAT tutors with individuals they think are even better qualified. Claire dutifully goes from tutor to tutor, hoping the latest one will do the trick. Unfortunately, these people raise her hopes and her anxiety—but not her SAT scores, which stubbornly refuse to budge.

In another effort to jump-start what they see as her flagging motivation, Claire's parents offer to pay her for good grades on her first quarter report card. Dangling this carrot backfires. Claire is indignant; she tells me, "They must be kidding! Do they really think that giving me twenty dollars for every A is going to make a difference?" The consensus among girls is confirmed by research: bribing brings mixed results. Although some students can be induced to perform better, others are put off. (Parents of girls who already enjoy learning might try the healthier strategy of challenging their intellectual curiosity rather than offering external rewards.)

For Claire, this tactic telegraphs in no uncertain terms that her parents are increasingly desperate to see her improve. Between keeping up with her class work, trying to do better on the SATs, staying in touch with her friends, doing preseason training for cheerleading, and dealing with her parents' anxiety, Claire is overwhelmed. Just before cheerleading begins, she decides to quit. "With all my classes, tutors, and other stuff," she tells me, "there's barely any time for me."

Before long, though, Claire regrets this decision. Not being with her cheerleading friends at practice every afternoon makes her feel lonely. Sometimes she feels left out in school when they talk about happenings or allude to inside jokes. And without the rigorous daily workouts she is used to, Claire gains weight. This distresses her no end. Girls who second-guess their abilities often become overly invested in their looks. Feeling fat is the final nail in the coffin of Claire's confidence.

While her parents focus on academics, Claire's deteriorating sense of self and growing discouragement take an even more devastating toll. Like ripples on a pond, the damage to her self-esteem soon spreads to other areas of her life. Combating her despair with the adrenaline rush of risk-taking behavior, I find out that she makes bad social choices. On weekends Claire goes from party to party, sometimes drinking excessively or experimenting with marijuana and Ecstasy. Until we address this in therapy, her substance use leads to casual sexual involvements that, at least momentarily, let her feel more desirable and powerful.

Hopeless to Measure Up

Like many square pegs, Claire fears never living up to the standards of her parents, teachers, or peers. She believes there is no pleasing the adults in her life:

> My parents keep pressuring me to get better grades. I'm really trying, but nothing is good enough for them. All they care about is getting into college. I really love them and want to make them happy, but I don't think I have the potential to do what they want me to do. Why don't they get that I'm not going to get into BU? I'm not that smart.

Teens read their parents' expectations with varying degrees of accuracy. Families tend to skirt around this issue rather than addressing it directly. Although girls frequently describe being "lectured" by their parents to be more motivated and to improve their grades, they rarely report sitting down and having open, heart-to-heart discussions that clarify precisely what each family member really expects.

In an e-mail, Chantelle poignantly describes this distress: "I get a lot of pressure from my parents to do really well. I guess they're expecting me to go to Harvard or something. I feel like a heavy burden is sitting on my chest whenever I think about school." Unless Chantelle is able to broach her perceptions with her parents, however, they may not know that their daughter is so stressed out in middle school—or why. Worse, they may never have the chance to correct her impressions. For all Chantelle knows, Harvard may never have crossed her parents' minds.

It is girls' assumptions about unspoken expectations that are so potentially harmful. Claire tells me that her parents always say, "You can do better!" "But," she asks, "what does that mean? I always get B's and C's and some A's. I've always gotten these grades. So why do they say that? This is who I am." Because they are vague about what she should be doing better, Claire is left with the impression that she is just not good enough. Like many girls, she is convinced that her parents are neither seeing nor accepting her for who she really is.

One day in therapy, Claire gets to the crux of the issue. She tells me, "My dad and I probably have totally different ideas of success. He envisioned me not to settle for being average." I suspected that Claire's parents, like many loving mothers and fathers, had overestimated her abilities. Even with gentle encouragement during our periodic sessions, it was hard for them to accept that she was an average student who probably wouldn't become an above-average student—no matter how gifted or diligent her tutors.

As if they are living in Garrison Keillor's imaginary town, Lake Wobegon, where every child is above average, many parents believe their daughters are extremely bright and therefore should be excelling. When girls get average grades, their parents conclude they must be underachieving and worry about possible learning or attention problems. In this competitive world, they are eager to fix any problems and bring their kids up to par.

For this reason, perhaps, I have found that a greater number of parents today are seeking psychoeducational assessments for their children—and not because they are doing poorly, but because they are not doing exceptionally well.

When I give parents feedback about testing results, I see that they are often painfully disappointed to learn that their kids are not superachievers, but merely average, or normal. Many would prefer to hear that their girls have specific learning disorders or attention deficits; that way, at least there is something to be remedied or medicated. Mothers and fathers want to think there is something they can do to help.

I often have to remind parents that native intelligence is not the most critical factor in determining whether people are successful. I see countless girls with superior IQs for whom school is a daily torment, as well as girls with supposedly average aptitude who excel in honors classes. That is because traditional cognitive tests do not measure motivation, curiosity, creativity, work habits, perseverance, or study skills—in other words, additional factors for success. Blessed with these vital gifts—or taught to develop them—girls better manage life's challenges and use their talents to the fullest.

Unfortunately, girls with more average cognitive abilities commonly feel pressured for above-average achievement. This is a bit like expecting kids to be taller or to have better eyesight, but it is more harmful. Although the bell-shaped curve of intelligence indicates that a full half of the population is average, girls who are not academic superstars often feel like inferior goods. Becky, who is in middle school, admits, "I think I'm gonna burst. The C on my report card proves I'm dumb."

We all have to ask ourselves whether we are unintentionally burdening girls with goals and expectations that are inappropriate for them. Recently a woman came to see me because she wanted to know why her daughter was having trouble in school. During the consultation, I asked about family background. Peggy burst into tears. "My sister has Stepford children," she told me. "Her girls are straight-A students—very smart, very athletic, very popular, class presidents." The unspoken contrast to her own teenager hung in the air until she added wistfully, "I try not to make comparisons."

I came to understand that Peggy still felt tortured by childhood competition between her sister and herself. Unlike her sister, the star of their family, Peggy was an uninspired student. Now she feared her daughter was going down the same path. This is one of a multitude of family dynamics causing parents to harbor hopes and dreams that are mismatched to their kids. In the same way, it is hard for Claire's parents to see that she is not cut from the same cloth as her more academically inclined brother and father. Pressures to excel that are not aligned with girls' true talents make them feel hopeless of measuring up and, therefore, diminish their confidence.

Plummeting Self-esteem

As the gulf between her performance and her parents' standards fails to narrow, Claire cannot help but feel increasingly inadequate. This is typical of teenage girls, who evaluate their progress according to others' reactions. It is not merely the achievements of good grades, making teams, and winning awards that make them feel good. Rather, it is the validation from their parents, teachers, and friends that makes all the difference. Girls in middle school and high school say they feel most successful when

+ "My parents tell me I am."
+ "I am complimented or praised."
+ "My teacher is happy with my work."
+ "I make someone happy."
+ "My parents and teachers are proud of me."
+ "I do well enough to impress even my mother."
+ "People are happy with me, whether or not my goal was successful."

Similarly, girls say they feel like the biggest failures when they get bad grades, lose their papers, or forget their assignments. But most of all, they feel unsuccessful when they sense others lose faith in them, when they are criticized, or when they think others don't believe they are doing their best, as demonstrated by these statements:

+ "I fail to live up to everyone's expectations."
+ "My teacher tells me to try harder."
+ "My parents are pissed about a B grade."
+ "I let someone down."
+ "My teacher doesn't have faith in me."
+ "My mother puts me down."
+ "I disappoint my parents and teachers."

Teens are utterly flattened by believing they will never be the individuals their parents, teachers, or peers want them to be. As their self-esteem deteriorates, they feel increasingly helpless to make things right. Girls who think they invariably disappoint people feel defeated even before they give themselves a chance. Their expectations of falling short become self-fulfilling prophecies. It is human nature to avoid attempting something when we think we have no chance of succeeding. Girls who feel undervalued don't try as hard. They typically make halfhearted efforts, slack off, or give up entirely.

That was Claire's experience of school: "Most of the time I rush through just to get done. I figure, why bother? I don't care as long as I don't have to think about it anymore." With this demoralized attitude, of course she does even more poorly in her classes. Then, in true cyclical fashion, she disengages further. To justify her mediocre performance, Claire complains that school is stupid and boring. What teens often mean by this is that *they* feel stupid and boring.

Girls who feel more valued, on the other hand, often make different choices. Whether they get affirmation from their parents, teachers, peers, or themselves, they feel empowered to undertake new or difficult endeavors. Even if they think they're not the best, they try out for school plays, sign up for challenging classes, take chances on different sports, and run for office. They do these things because they think they can.

A Deteriorating Parent-Teen Relationship

Over time, constant friction about academics, as well as the inferred criticism and rejection, increasingly frays the bonds between square pegs and their parents. Claire is no exception. By keeping her despair and secret life hidden, she prevents her parents from truly understanding her. Although many mothers and fathers I work with in counseling are able to change their thinking and shift their expectations to be more in line with their daughters' inclinations, it was hard for Claire's parents to let go of their dream.

Daily conflicts not only erode the good will in parent-teen relationships, but also make it hard for girls to trust and ask for help when they need it. Under these conditions too, some teens begin to question—and sometimes reject—their parents' values. A few decide to rebel.

Erosion of Trust. Fortunately, unlike many undervalued girls, Claire does not fall into the trap of hiding bad grades, progress notices, or report cards to avoid disappointing her parents. "I was tempted to lie when I got a D. I wanted to cover it up, I was so desperate," she tells me. "One of my best friends, CJ, didn't tell her mom about her second semester report card. Her mom asks her every day, and she keeps on lying." But having tested the waters with a low math grade, Claire learned that her parents are more likely to help her than to punish her. She concludes, "I don't have to lie."

Still, with the tension in her family, Claire despairs of getting the support she needs when she is confused about her work. Sensing her father's nervous energy about achievement, she is filled with anxiety on the rare occasions when she approaches him. His overeagerness puts her off. She explains, "Sometimes I'm afraid to ask him a question because then I'll get an hour-long answer, and it'll be like speaking gibberish." As with many undervalued girls, when Claire doesn't come asking for help, her parents interpret this as further proof of her apathy.

Less Eager to Please. When girls feel distant from their parents or are mired in daily conflict, they are also less apt to follow their guidelines. As one of the girls in my focus group explained:

> *It has to do with the relationship between parent and kid. If it's a good relationship, they'll want their approval, and they'll try to do better. If they don't get along, they won't try as hard because they don't care what their parents think. My mother and I don't get along. She's always picking at me.*

We're always fighting. She doesn't want to hear what I have
to say, so I kind of just ignore her.

For the same reason, girls who feel out of place and unsuccessful in school find themselves clashing with their teachers. Sarah, a
freshman, told me, "My teacher's not really interested in my ideas.
When I write what I think—and not what she wants to hear—she
gives me bad grades. So I basically have a choice. I'm not going to
feed her back what she wants to hear just to get the A." More con-
formity is needed for an adolescent to do well in high school than
most adults have to muster in their lives.

Teens who feel inadequate as a result of being square pegs have
few options. Unless they challenge the values and goals of their
parents or teachers, they become critical of themselves. To avoid
further damaging their already shaky confidence, teenage girls
are understandably reluctant to admit their faults. So they use
their new, higher-level reasoning skills to analyze their parents'
and teachers' beliefs about success. They scrutinize adults' values
and motivations, and are delighted to discover any inconsistency
or hypocrisy that can let them off the hook.

For example, as Claire becomes increasingly aware of her unhappiness and sense of not fitting in, this is exactly what she does.
The anger that had been self-directed is now turned toward her
parents. "For seventeen years," she tells me, "I've heard them say
how they think I can be doing better. If I get a B, my dad always
says to me, 'Where there's a will, there's an A.'" She sighs and rolls
her eyes. "And, oh, here's another helpful one," she says sarcastically. "'Try your best. Then try harder!'" Mimicking the homilies
that filled her childhood, Claire bristles with resentment.

The same issues affect sports. She says, "Even though my parents worked, they were totally there for me and my brother in
school and sports. They always went to our games and pointed out
stuff we could do to improve." The message "We support you" felt

good to her. But as soon as her parents recognized her potential as an athlete, their involvement began to feel critical. The extra coaching in T-ball, private tennis lessons, and premier soccer clinics said to her, "Maybe you can be great at this." No longer was it enough for Claire to play sports, or even to play well. "All of a sudden I had to show them I could be the best," she says. "And that's what they expect in everything."

Like all teenagers, Claire also observes how her parents live their own lives. To guard against finding fault with herself, she now critiques them, eager to assign blame. Her father, an electrical engineer, is high-strung and exacting. "He's always so uptight," Claire says, "he never just relaxes or chills." Her mother is equally intense; a successful partner in an Internet company, she is known for her methodical style. "Both of my parents admit they're overachievers. They are always so serious, so focused on this goal or that goal." Claire is determined to put herself in a whole different category, in part to rid herself of their expectations.

Mounting Rebellion. Some teens begin to rebel against what they see as their parents' overzealous efforts to orchestrate their success. For example, girls tell me of mothers or fathers insisting that they take Spanish instead of French, deciding they shouldn't drop honors science, or picking out their prom dates. Not only do girls dislike being micromanaged, but they are also offended by the implication that their parents find them incapable of making such decisions on their own. Feeling pushed to achieve, especially in directions that seem wrong or uncomfortable for them, many girls stubbornly push back.

A high school senior who is filling out college applications tells me, "My parents want to be very involved. They'd like to make decisions for me, tell me what I'm supposed to be working toward. This gives me the urge to do badly. It makes you want to rebel." Similarly, Deanna says, "A lot of times, my parents tell me to do something before I can do something else. So I give up the thing I want to do. I just don't want to feel like somebody is controlling me."

In fact, by digging in their heels, some girls sabotage their own success just to make their point. Nan, for example, who is now in college, tells of a self-defeating power struggle with her parents during high school. "They were always on my case. I couldn't take it. If they told me I should do math first, I purposely did it last. When they said I needed quiet to study, I kept my stereo blasting." Nan felt obligated to keep up this oppositional behavior and improved only after she got a letter informing her that she couldn't play basketball until she brought up her GPA.

Girls who feel like square pegs also use rebellion as a refusal to become their parents' emblems of success. Their behavior asserts "I will do anything and everything to prove that I am my own person." Although girls believe that taking this stance proves their autonomy, ironically it does the opposite. Making decisions merely because they are polar opposite of their parents' wishes actually demonstrates their dependency. What is more damaging is that reacting to their parents' goals leaves girls little room to discover their own.

HELPING SQUARE PEGS

Parents can establish two effective guidelines for reducing girls' pressure to measure up: First, they must be mindful of their powerful influence, and second, they must be willing to examine, and possibly modify, their interactions with their daughters about achievement. Building on these fundamentals, the following strategies are appropriate for all girls, but especially for those at risk for feeling like square pegs.

► Reduce Pressure

The most potent antidote to your daughter's stress may be the alleviation of your own. Use whatever strategy usually works for you. Realizing that there are many paths to success may help you to come to terms with your daughter's struggles. You may also remain calmer if you attend to what is going on in the moment rather than making anxious projections about her future or harping on her past failures. Then you will be in a better position to do everything possible to relieve the pressure she is experiencing.

The benefits of this approach are enormous. Jasmine's guidance counselor, for example, marvels that she seems entirely comfortable in taking a route that is so different from that of her classmates. "Jasmine is a highflier," she tells me, "but she is always her own person." The reason for this, her guidance counselor tells me, lies in her parents' attitude: "She was brought up that way. It all depends on the kind of acceptance girls enjoy at home. Jasmine feels unqualified acceptance. Somebody isn't going to fuss about her getting a B. Home is safe."

► Avoid Comparisons

No matter how tempting, refrain from comparing your daughter unfavorably to siblings, friends, or classmates who look more successful. Not only won't this help your daughter, but also your judgments may turn out to be wrong. You have no idea if these kids' talents or achievements will actually pay off later or what struggles they may be hiding beneath their outward accomplishments.

▶ Monitor Your Behavior

Be aware of the messages you convey through your behavior. Teens are adept at differentiating between parental efforts that are truly designed to help them and those that are based on other, less beneficial motives. Gabriella gives me this example:

> *My dad travels a lot, and when he calls up, he asks stuff like "What did you read today?" or "Was it interesting?" or "What was your favorite class?" He wants to hear what I think. I feel sorry for my best friend. Her father travels all the time too, but when he calls her up, he's like, "Fax me a paragraph about the book you're reading." She hates that, 'cause it's like another homework assignment, only her father's gonna be grading it according to how he thinks she should be doing it.*

▶ Discover Their Passions

Develop an open mind about the shape of success. When parents are not intent upon seeing specific benchmarks or outcomes, they give daughters an extraordinary gift: freedom from having to choose whether to please others or to follow their own dreams. Know when your daughter wants to be the social director rather than the captain of the ship, the nurse instead of the neurosurgeon, or the ballerina rather than the dance teacher. Then help her pursue those passions in every way possible, whether that means voice lessons, acting classes, art camp, or writing workshops.

In the early spring of her junior year, Claire tells me that she wants to get a part-time job in her favorite clothing store, which caters to style-conscious young teens. At first her parents refuse because they fear that having less time to do her homework will be disastrous. But with my support, Claire presents her parents with compelling reasons why the job would be good for her. They agree to let her work on the condition that she must quit if her school-work suffers.

Almost at once it is obvious that Claire has found her calling. She sees that she is a natural. Her flair for fashion, knack for orga-nization and efficiency, and great people skills have not been assets in geometry or chemistry, but they earn glowing praise and respect from her new employers. Claire's young customers adore her; she has a knack for putting together their outfits and accessories and making them feel special in the process. Earning her own money makes Claire feel more grown up. But it is feeling valued and see-ing her skills recognized and appreciated that eventually lift her mood.

For the first time, Claire begins to imagine a future after high school. She dares to think about a career in retail, merchandising, or design. Getting through high school suddenly has purpose. Al-though she doesn't become an A student, Claire buckles down with a new enthusiasm that is reflected by her end-of-year grades. Throughout the spring, I am pleased and relieved to see that her growing confidence has encouraged her to take better care of her-self in her social life. After much discussion in therapy, she decides to stop using drugs and hooking up with boys.

► Relinquish Inappropriate Control

It is difficult for parents to resist the urge to make a B student into an A student, an average athlete into a superstar, or a reserved girl into a popular leader. It is all too easy to think, "If only . . ." and to offer whatever remedies they see fit. Yet to encourage any daughter's burgeoning individuality, especially one who feels undervalued, it is necessary to stop trying to control her life. Remind yourself that all kids have a right to focus on their own talents and decide their own futures.

Square pegs can be most resilient to stress when their mothers and fathers don't try to transform them into round pegs. These parents accept that their daughters' futures are not opportunities to rewrite their own histories or to experience vicarious glory. Being put in charge of their own lives liberates girls like nothing else. However, it is often difficult for parents to let go of their own expectations.

Morgan, a student in a small high school just outside a major city, was at an impasse with her parents because of their determination to make her into a tennis great. She tells me, "I really wanted to do track, but my dad made me try out for varsity tennis. I've been playing since I was four. My parents play, and they've been giving me lessons forever. They're hoping I'll be recruited for college. They'd really love a tennis scholarship. I don't know. I think I just don't love tennis as much as they want me to."

Despite her obvious skill, Morgan's heart isn't in the sport. Her coach probably senses her ambivalence. Before the tennis team is to play its biggest rival, the roster of girls who will compete is posted. When Morgan is not chosen, her father is upset. "He wants me to take private lessons," she tells me. "But I don't think that's a good idea. What if I still don't get to play? It'll be a big waste of money. Or what if I mess up and my team loses?"

Morgan tells me she feels like a puppet on strings. "My mom played tennis in high school until her knee went out. She should have been the tennis star." Because of her family's need to see *her* become the tennis star, Morgan feels obligated to fulfill their dream. She resents her parents making these decisions for her, and feels deprived of the chance to see if track would work out for her.

Fortunately, with counseling her father becomes more receptive to seeing her viewpoint. He comes to acknowledge that she has a right to pursue her own path, even to "squander her talent" if she chooses. Although it is hard to break his old habits, he makes a concerted effort to stop offering extra tennis lessons and asking her to practice with him. As he pulls back, Morgan finds that she enjoys being on the team more than she had thought. Although she is still not sure whether she would like track better, she feels more comfortable talking to her parents—and more confident that they hear her. Morgan is greatly relieved by their implicit permission for her to be herself.

▶ Maintain Positive Relationships

In a myriad of ways, having close relationships with parents benefits all stressed-out girls. But for girls vulnerable to feeling like square pegs, this is key for resiliency. Now a college sophomore, Miranda realizes that until her parents came to terms with the fact that she was different from the rest of her highly achieving family, she had been handicapped by their continual disappointment and the tension that ensued.

Though she wanted to follow her siblings to Ivy League colleges, Miranda could never emulate their high school studying regimen. She did the bare minimum to get by. Seeing her report cards, her alarmed parents considered her lazy and even disloyal. Miranda lied to them about her incomplete work "partly so they'd get off my back and partly 'cause I didn't want to face up to what I was doing." She now admits that it was the overwhelming desire to avoid seeing herself as the "loser" of her family that kept her from asking for the help she knew she needed.

Miranda and her parents eventually came to see that although she was smart (she got nearly perfect SAT scores), she was a different sort of scholar from her sister and brother. Although she disliked memorizing history facts, she stayed most informed about current events by reading the *New York Times* every day cover to cover. Miranda's adviser helped her parents to see that she needed a different educational path. Unlike her siblings, she did better when she avoided time-consuming, stressful AP and honors classes in favor of less demanding and more intriguing courses.

To Miranda's surprise, picking the right courses jump-started her motivation and, ultimately, her grades. She bravely applied to her favorite college, which was considered a reach, and was accepted on an early decision basis.

▶ Consider Other Options

Many times, girls who feel like square pegs feel stuck. They certainly can't change their families, and they often can't change their schools. But for teens who do have options, parents might consider whether their daughters would be better off in a different environment—whether it is school or camp or jazz class—with which they are better matched. Although this issue is discussed more generally in Chapter 10, a transfer can transform some undervalued girls. They suddenly feel like they fit in—and they excel.

One example is Risa, a high school freshman I evaluated recently. Although she did well in other subjects, Risa struggled every year in math because of a profound learning disability. She accepted her need to work harder to understand math concepts, but took pride in being recognized as the best artist in her grade. The new private school where she had started, with its rather rigorous and rigid curriculum, became a nightmare. Not only was her art not appreciated, but without support to learn in her own way, Risa became increasingly demoralized. Fortunately, her parents saw an opportunity. They moved to another state where they enrolled her in a high school for the creative arts.

In a way, Claire's story had a similar outcome. Though she ended therapy at the beginning of her senior year, I received a follow-up call from her mother the following fall. Claire had not been accepted at BU. Instead, she was attending a smaller, less competitive college nearby. Within the first weeks of school, her mother marveled, Claire had settled in, met her boyfriend, and was actually excited about her classes. As I heard this update, I thought how fortunate Claire was to end up at a school that allowed her, finally, to experience being a square peg in a square hole.

Whenever parents can reduce stress, maintain broad ideas about success, and give up inappropriate control over the details in their daughters' lives, girls are best able to cope with being different from their families or classmates. They are less likely to interpret their uniqueness negatively and to feel like misfits. When their parents and teachers honor their individuality, these girls gain the confidence, self-reliance, and genuineness that arise from pursuing their real passions—in their own ways, and in their own time.

CHAPTER 6

Desperate for Acceptance: Insecure Girls

The winds of adolescence usually usher in stronger social desires. In middle school and high school, where peer acceptance is often more elusive than academic excellence, stressed-out girls find it even harder to navigate relationships. All their vulnerabilities—whether they feel undervalued, are in the midst of transitions, are characteristically perfectionistic, or are distracted by personal troubles—shape their interactions with classmates and teachers in predictable ways.

For insecure teens, however, the main problem *is* their relationships. Specifically, they are desperate to feel accepted by others outside their families. This preoccupation with getting approval from peers or adults insidiously affects many areas of their lives, chipping away at their self-esteem, their performance, and sometimes their success.

It is not that teen girls ever feel completely assured that their friendships will stay on an even keel, much less last forever. All girls are vulnerable to periodic feelings of insecurity. How confident your daughter feels in her closest relationships will probably vacillate throughout her teen years, fluctuating along with notoriously fickle social tides. In fact, these shifts in social harmony may be secretly responsible for many of the temporary ups and downs you observe in her mood and general functioning during her middle school and high school years. But this chapter addresses the girls with chronic insecurity—and the toll it takes on their everyday adolescent experience.

The Benefits of Social Connectedness

Teens who are able to maintain satisfying peer relationships benefit in many ways. At a minimum, they can count on seeing friendly faces in their classes and are assured of being welcomed at a cafeteria table. They worry less about feeling awkward or self-conscious as a result of being alone. The Alfred P. Sloan Study of Youth and Social Development, a national longitudinal study of more than twelve hundred middle and high school students conducted during a five-year period, found that teenagers who felt connected with others reported higher self-esteem and were generally happier and more motivated.

Especially for girls, maintaining close relationships translates into a sense of accomplishment. As previously mentioned, teen girls (far more than their male classmates) base their triumphs and failures not just on grades and scores and other accolades, but, more important, on how they affect the people they value most. In my study, for example, girls spoke of feeling most successful when

- ✦ "I show someone how to do something I know how to do."
- ✦ "I say something that has made a person happy."
- ✦ "My status with friends is great."
- ✦ "I help someone who is upset."
- ✦ "I do good deeds, am a good friend, and am a good daughter."
- ✦ "I help another to succeed."

+ "I put a smile on someone's face."
+ "I calm down a friend who is stressed or having a dilemma."

Recent advances in science corroborate that feelings directly affect achievement. According to Daniel Goleman, author of *Emotional Intelligence*, being in a cheerful mood or laughing improves cognitive abilities by enabling people to think more broadly and flexibly. When teen girls are in good spirits, they can be more creative, solve problems more effectively, and anticipate the consequences of their decisions. The academic benefits of feeling comfortable and secure in the classroom should not be overlooked.

In addition, there are practical perks that contribute to girls' success. Socially connected students are more comfortable approaching their teachers for help. They are more likely to be chosen for group tasks, to study together, to share research material, to borrow forgotten books, and to call a classmate to clarify confusing assignments. They support each other in persisting with tasks that are difficult or tedious. When they can commiserate with each other about their teachers' idiosyncrasies, they bond and blow off steam. A positive attitude and acceptance by peers go a long way in school.

Resilient girls seem better able to handle interpersonal challenges than more insecure teens. Perhaps they develop better social skills that give them an edge in handling difficult people and complex social situations. Confidence may also make them withstand pressures for acceptance. These girls are usually more philosophical about the fact that not everyone will like them and that friendships inevitably change over time. Edy wrote in an e-mail about keeping social issues in perspective:

Most of the peer pressure at my school is about being popular, pretty, and perfect. Generally it comes from the girls who think they are popular, pretty, and perfect. Me, well, I'm not really any of these. At one time I always wanted to be popular and pretty. I thought that people would like me more if I was like this. But then I realized that I didn't have to be popular to have friends and have a happy life.

The Risks of Insecurity

What is important for adults to recognize is that teens who agonize about their acceptance go through their school days differently from their more secure classmates. Eager for evidence that they are passing muster, they become highly alert to cues about how others perceive them. Insecure girls constantly monitor their looks and actions to make sure they fit in, and then look to others for confirmation. With the precision of statisticians, they track the subtlest fluctuations in classmates' facial expressions as well as teachers' moods and behavior to gauge whether or not they are judged to be acceptable.

This preoccupation with where they stand with teachers and peers takes its toll, draining these teens' energy. Even when they enjoy their school work and activities, it may be hard to give their all. Of course, no matter their façade, girls often keep their underlying insecurity hidden. What adults may see are girls who are either outwardly hypersocial, precocious, and frantically busy—or immature and isolated. Yet the common thread linking these insecure girls is that they are not doing as well as possible.

AMY

A Crisis in the Making

When Amy's mother calls to ask for an appointment, the urgency in her voice is unmistakable. Gladys begins by telling me that Amy, her only child, "has so much promise, yet she's wasting it—and for what?" Although she was tested and identified as gifted, Amy is doing even worse in seventh grade than she did the year before. Not only has school been relegated to a back burner, but there are also alarming new signs of trouble. "All Amy does is sit in her room on the computer," Gladys says. "She talks to her friends online day and night. I can't get her off. It's not healthy; it's like she's addicted. And she thinks she's fat. She's not, but I think she's trying to lose weight."

The comments on Amy's most recent report card add to Gladys's concerns. When she reads that Amy "comes unprepared to class" and "needs to participate more in class discussions," she calls her guidance counselor to get more information. Amy's teachers report that she is shy and apathetic. She doesn't contribute or ask questions. When called upon, she mumbles. Gladys is stunned. Amy has always been one of the more active students, eager to be in the thick of things and voice her opinions. It is as if the guidance counselor is describing someone else's daughter. More than anything, this prompts Gladys to wonder what is going on and bring Amy for help.

The Distress of Disconnection

When she arrives at my office, I notice at once that Amy looks different from other girls her age. Although she is as physically mature, there is a lack of sophistication about her. Amy also looks somewhat unkempt. She is wearing cargo pants that are the rage, but they are tight around her waist, too short, and clash with her plaid blouse. Perhaps most striking, her dark hair falls unevenly down her back in long, tangled strands. It is likely that middle schoolers would see Amy as unusual.

In our first discussion, she denies having any problems. Amy tells me that she has "tons of friends in school." When I ask about academics, she replies indifferently, "I'm doing okay." The only thing bothering her is her parents. "I don't know why they're flipping out," she complains. "I said I'd bring up my grades." That Amy plays down her difficulties, is nonchalant about her parents' growing alarm, and believes her grades will magically improve does nothing to allay her mother's fears. In fact, Gladys now worries that Amy could be hiding something more ominous.

It turns out that Amy's most well-kept secret is the extent of her distress. During her fourth appointment, she promptly bursts into tears. The session is filled with one heartbreaking confession after the next. Amy's parents and teachers have no idea how ostracized she feels in school. "The girls are so mean!" she sobs. "They think I'm a loser because I don't wear tight clothes. But I don't want to get a bad reputation. This one girl, Tammy, is always going, 'Your top doesn't match' or 'Those sneakers are so lame.' I feel like a freak. Sometimes I think everybody hates me."

Later on I ask Amy how all of this is affecting her work. She rattles off a laundry list of problems. When the girl who sits next to her in math ignores her, it is hard to pay attention to what the teacher is saying. She is too upset by the look another girl gave her (if she *did* give her a look) to concentrate on a French pop quiz. When her supposed friend chooses another girl as a lab partner, she is convinced she will fail science.

Girls are often just as eager for signs of acceptance from their teachers. The less secure they are, in fact, the more they need a personal connection with their teachers in order to thrive in school. Many teens tune into their teachers' moods and listen for hints of approval or disappointment much in the same way they scrutinize their peers.

Amy tells me about a teacher "who was not supportive at all. Any time I'd ask a question, she'd just walk away from me. Another time, this teacher's pet forgot a book in her locker. She asks to get the book. When I asked the same thing, the teacher got mad at me." Another insulted her. "Why did my teacher say we had a lot more to cover?" she asks. "Does he think I'm slacking off or something? I just skipped one little reading assignment! I hate him!"

It is clear that she views her teacher's comments through the distorted lens of her own supersensitivity. Girls want their teachers to respect them, to listen to them, and, above all, to protect them from humiliation. When these conditions for security are met, they are more likely to make an effort. It is a self-fulfilling prophecy, then, that teens who feel well regarded by their teachers have a leg up on their less assured classmates.

When girls claim "I hate my teacher," this is usually code for "I'm not doing well in that class." More often than not, the primary cause is not difficulty with the subject matter, but rather a fault in the student-teacher connection. Girls typically believe the teacher is treating them unfairly, is not specifying their expectations, or simply does not like them. For insecure middle or high school girls, this can be a recipe for failure.

As Amy recites her complaints, she sounds increasingly frantic. As she nears the limit of what she can tolerate, it is clear why it is hard for her to get through her day.

> *It's stressful in middle school because besides passing all of my classes, you feel like people are always judging you. You feel like you have to look all presentable, like you have to take three hours to do your hair. Every day, people talk about what you're wearing and what you're saying. My teachers are always judging me every minute. I can't stand it anymore!*

For insecure girls, every school day is a unit test—or perhaps a final exam—assessing whether they are accepted and, more important, acceptable. As Amy describes, "Sometimes when my friends get on the hot lunch line and don't wait for me, I think, 'I'm a dork, nobody likes me.' Then, if my friends save me a seat at lunch, I'm like, 'Okay, you're all right.'" Sensing approval becomes a moment-by-moment litmus test of self-worth for insecure girls.

Adults may not appreciate how devastating this can be. One senior I interviewed told me it is still painful for her to recall the despair she experienced earlier in high school. "As a sophomore, I hated school. I did not feel like myself, ever," she said. "I spent days in bed because school wasn't a place that I felt safe. I could never be myself or express myself properly." Like many insecure girls, she developed physical symptoms that excused her absences from school, but the real diagnosis was hidden social angst.

Research consistently demonstrates that social adjustment affects students' success. According to psychologist Kathryn Wentzel of the University of Maryland and her colleagues, those with close, reciprocal friendships at the beginning of sixth grade made a better adjustment to middle school—and that advantage persisted even two years later in eighth grade. Friendless students, on the other hand, reported higher levels of emotional distress and sadness and lower self-esteem.

Similarly, psychologist Roy Baumeister of Case Western Reserve University found a relationship between social acceptance and cognitive abilities. Specifically, feeling rejected leads to many negative behaviors such as aggression, cheating, and procrastination. Social exclusion also makes it harder for students to be self-disciplined and to set priorities. Remarkably, these students even score more poorly on intelligence tests. The self-denigration that accompanies social rejection seems to undermine thinking.

Amy's social isolation is at the heart of her difficulties. Although her parents believe her when she says that she has "tons of friends," in reality there are only a couple of girls who talk to her in class or in the hall. During our sessions, she confided that despite her non-stop instant messaging with schoolmates she barely knows, she has not a single real friend. Amy has no one to confide in when she is upset. No one makes her feel valued by calling her to ask for advice. She is not included in after-school plans, and has not been invited to a single birthday party this year. No wonder she is feeling estranged, adrift, and increasingly discouraged. Amy's "addiction" to online messaging provides her only contact with peers outside of school.

Unfortunately, it is difficult for Amy's parents to empathize with her longing to be included and her distress about being ignored. They see her classmates as trashy. Like all parents, their judgments are shaped by their own backgrounds. As teens, neither of Amy's parents was well connected or attuned to their own peer culture. In fact, both parents had been rather isolated during their adolescent years. "Why is this so important to her?" Gladys challenges me, "and who'll even care about this in ten years? We both survived. Amy's future is at stake now. She can't let these kids pull her down."

At first, they believe that limiting their daughter's computer privileges will solve her problems. Although it is true that Amy needs to manage her time better, she feels as if her parents have cut off her oxygen supply. Feeling deprived of any connection to her peers, no matter how tenuous, she becomes highly anxious about "showing my face in school." To cover her fears, which embarrass her, she is infuriated with her parents and determined to blame them. As Amy's mood shifts unpredictably from apathy to indifference to defiance, the family seems to lose its bearings.

A History of Social Woes

Although Amy and her parents feel that this crisis comes from nowhere, her past history suggests otherwise. Most insecure teens have endured earlier painful losses or traumatic social events. Some have limited interpersonal skills that prevent them from coping well. Amy felt like the odd girl out during fifth grade, when she transferred from private school to a public school populated by neighborhood students who had known each other since kindergarten. Entering a large middle school the following year, she felt overwhelmed by the influx of new sixth graders from four different elementary schools. Unlike girls in transition, Amy's social insecurity becomes chronic.

While meeting new kids thrills many girls, Amy feels threatened whenever girls get together with other friends. This possessiveness is off-putting; one by one her new friends distance themselves from her. One incident is especially hurtful. "Ariel just dropped me without saying a thing," Amy says. "She started ignoring me so she could be friends with these popular girls that we hate because they're such snobs." Devastated by this betrayal, Amy limps through the rest of the school year feeling rebuffed and alone, too self-conscious to risk approaching girls in other groups.

Although feeling accepted is paramount for most teens, for insecure girls this goal becomes the top priority. Determined to find at least one person whom she can connect with and call a friend, Amy spends inordinate time trying to decipher unspoken social rules. She says evenly, "I know from personal experience that girls at my school are very judgmental. Everybody wants to fit in, but not all girls do. Us girls feel that if we aren't pretty or popular, we won't fit in with anybody. We want the most popular girls to like us because then the other girls will start to like us more."

The Fallout of Insecurity

Self-consciousness. Attributing their own self-consciousness to others, insecure girls usually believe that other people dissect them—their appearance, clothing, actions, and friendships—as intensely as they scrutinize themselves. Amy constantly feels examined and critiqued. But much as mirrors can distort images in unflattering ways, when girls look to others for approval they often see exaggerated flaws reflected back to them.

One social rule of thumb during the teenage years is to avoid standing out in the crowd because that attracts negative attention. Insecure girls try to blend in to avoid yet another social liability. Thus, teens who are eager for acceptance don't want to be too smart, too dumb, too skinny, too much of a loser, too fat, too much of a jock, too uncoordinated, too sexy, too ugly, too babyish, too pretty, or too successful. Any one of these undesirable labels might cast them into social oblivion.

The morning I visit one school, the girls are in a state because the roster of this year's basketball team will be posted later in the afternoon. They are all obsessing about whether they will be chosen. What if you don't make the team? I ask these anxious girls. In response, I don't hear about fears of missing out on playing their favorite sport or wanting to be part of a team. "Well, then I'd have to tell everyone" was their usual answer. "I'll be humiliated."

It is easy to take lightly the impact of seemingly minor embarrassing moments. Yet I have learned that when they occur in public, many incidents become imbued with the emotional intensity of traumas. In my surveys of teens' worst school experiences, they universally report mundane episodes of crying, falling down, slipping, tripping, or dropping something. Many speak of rumors circulating about them or someone revealing the identity of their crush. One wrote, "When I yelled 'No!' in the cafeteria and everyone looked at me." Another said, "I fell down a flight of stairs and my laptop hit me over the head, my knees bled through my white tights, and all the seniors laughed at me."

Too Cool for School. For the same reasons, standing out at either end of the intellectual continuum—being either too smart or not smart enough—frightens insecure girls. It is hard to strike a balance between being competent and powerful on the one hand, and being accepted on the other. Lynne says that in her high school "the highly competitive kids push you by poking fun if you're not as good as they are. And then if you come out on top, you're labeled a teacher's pet. So where I'm from, you'd better blend in but stay on top." She looks contemplative as she pauses. "Weird, huh?"

Whether or not high achievers are seen as socially acceptable varies by school, by community, and also by the chemistry of students making up each class. But an inverse relationship between popularity and achievement is not uncommon in middle school. According to a Girls Inc. survey, 44 percent of girls say the smartest girls in school are not popular. Amy agrees: "A lot of smarter people hang out together and people who slack off hang together, and people in the middle hang out. People in the middle or those not as smart are more popular than those who are."

What this means for Amy is that "school is very stressing because if you let it be known that you actually like school, you'll be branded a dork forever." Unconsciously, at least, this belief may be preventing her from succeeding despite her intellectual gifts. She is aware of how her peers in middle school react. "I used to love it when my teachers said, 'I wish I had more kids like you,' but sometimes when I raise my hand to answer a question, kids look at me like I have eight heads."

Amy also recalls that her focus on schoolwork used to create tension with the girls she attempted to befriend in sixth grade. "Sometimes this girl would ask me why I didn't go somewhere Friday night, like skating or to a party. I always said I was busy or I had to do my homework. It was true, but they couldn't understand because they didn't care about grades so much and hardly did their homework. They thought I was lying."

Self-doubt and Inhibition Tremendous self-doubt lies at the core of many of these detrimental changes in attitude and behavior. It is why Amy second-guesses everything she says and does in school. "Today I started thinking that maybe I laugh too much. I used to think that would be good. Kids would see me as a fun person. But today I felt like maybe I was acting too silly. Kim was looking at me like I was stupid or something." Amy is constantly thinking about whether her behavior is attractive or repulsive to her peers.

As she enters classrooms, passes through hallways, and negotiates the cafeteria, she is plagued by skeptical voices playing over and over again in her head. She explains, "You see other people and wonder, 'Why don't I look like them? Is something wrong with me? Do I need to buy that T-shirt to be cool?'" Feeling at sea, Amy confesses: "I always wonder," she nearly whispers, "do girls who talk to me *really* like me?"

Insecure girls are especially intimidated by boys, who tend to be more overtly competitive in the classroom. Michaela, for example, describes the dynamics in her tenth-grade chemistry class:

It was male dominated. I didn't raise my hand all semester. This group of guys was competitive with each other. "What did you get? Oh, you're so dumb that you missed that!" They would point out everybody's weakness. It was scary. I didn't do as well as I did the first semester. You're afraid they might say something or joke around if you said something dumb. They may not take it personally, but I would if they did it to me.

Occasionally, girls get caught up in class discussions despite themselves. When they feel passionate about something, they hear themselves blurting out answers or opinions. Afterward, however, they describe ruminating about whether they made fools of themselves. After such indiscretions, in fact, some girls demur by apologizing for having a different viewpoint—or perhaps for having the temerity to articulate it.

Alternatively, some girls deal with social insecurity by adopting a persona of imperturbability. They monopolize classroom discussions, daring others to disagree, or get nasty or hostile about their peers' ideas. These girls act as if they have bees in their bonnets. Rosa, for example, is known for her feisty reaction to the know-it-alls in her classes. She looks up from the homework she is finishing in an ongoing high school focus group one morning and says, "It gets me mad. I just want to prove them wrong, so you figure out something they don't know . . ."

"If I knew all that," says her friend Heidi, laughing, "I'd probably raise my hand that much too, and then other people would probably be annoyed." She is alluding to a dilemma that is all too common among teens. When it comes to participating in class, insecure girls walk that same fine line between not being enough and being too much. They are afraid of both extremes: not saying enough and saying too much.

Yet teachers often penalize girls for keeping quiet. As with Amy, this shows up in their class participation grades and in the comments on their report cards. Many times their silence prompts teachers to think of them as less motivated, less knowledgeable, and less enthusiastic about learning than their more involved and outspoken peers. Insecure teens pick up on their teachers' disapproval. Then, in cyclical fashion, they are even more hesitant to speak up and have fewer opportunities to feel good about themselves when their contributions are publicly recognized and praised.

Academic Inhibition. In the classroom, girls in the lower grades find it easier to raise their hands and answer questions because they are socialized to please their teachers. In adolescence, however, girls often become too self-conscious to speak up. Insecure girls are hypersensitive to potential ridicule. They believe everyone is examining them, analyzing how they act and what they know, and waiting for them to mess up. One wrong move—or one stupid answer—and they will be humiliated. As Amy describes:

> *Teachers are thinking all this stuff about what you're doing. Whether we're doing our work, getting to class on time, whether we've got the stuff we're supposed to have, if we're participating enough—or maybe we're talking too much. And then other kids give you these looks, like you're dumb. It puts kids under a lot of pressure.*

When girls are surveyed, in fact, humiliation is frequently responsible for their worst school experiences. In class, they are embarrassed by being singled out or having their weakness revealed to their peers. As one teen reports, "My paper was used as an example of what not to do."

Another girl tells our focus group about feeling terrible when she was the only one in her class to get a poor grade. "I had a math teacher who announced that we're going to have a party if everyone got an A. Then she said no, we're not having the party because one person did really badly." She pauses. "I was the one who got the D. I felt so horrible, I wanted to drop out of class."

Her friend, who is sitting next to her, sympathizes. "Yeah, if you don't have your homework, our teacher asks where it is. He says it in front of the class, and the whole class goes silent and the whole class stares at you. Everybody stares at you." Another girl chimes in, "My teacher reads everyone's grades out loud. It's so embarrassing!"

They are now on a roll. Urged on by one another's candor, every girl at the table offers an example of a teacher whose behavior humiliated them. The ease with which they rattle off these incidents speaks volumes about their powerful impact. Devalued and insulted, girls keep their distress to themselves. They feel too uncomfortable to expose themselves to their classmates or teachers.

To avoid drawing attention to themselves and possibly risking exposure, insecure teens decide to play it safe. Rather than saying things out loud and putting them out there for other people to criticize, they fade into the background. They sit quietly, looking down at their desks, and hope their teachers don't call on them. Rarely do they speak up spontaneously. "I don't trust people," declares Amy. "It takes me awhile. When we just learn something, I don't raise my hand. It takes awhile to get in my head." She will speak only "when I'm totally sure I know what I'm talking about."

Eating Issues. Self-consciousness especially soars at the lunch table. After several months, Amy tells me that she feels "weird" eating french fries when she knows she's fat. She thinks that kids must be secretly thinking, "Why is she eating fries when she needs to lose weight?" This theme emerges all too often in my discussions with teen girls.

When I learn from my survey that students in high school generally enjoy their free periods more than lunch, initially I think that girls are struggling with the social pressures of the cafeteria, such as with whom they want to sit and whether to exclude kids they don't like from their table. But when I ask the junior girls in my focus group for their interpretation of this finding, I am surprised by what I hear.

"Oh, lots of girls have eating disabilities," one girl explains casually, as if this were common knowledge. "They're worried about their weight, and everybody is looking at them."

"Everyone wants to be thin, but it doesn't really matter that much. It's not like you have to be thin," argues Nell, minimizing how important body image is among her friends.

"Oh, but being fat or slutty humiliates you, it obliterates you," Marcie responds. "Everybody shuns fat people." She puts girls who cannot control their urges for food in the same category as those who hunger for sex.

In fact, social acceptance and physical attraction—especially being slender—are inextricably linked. According to a Girls Inc. study, 48 percent of girls believe the most popular girls in school are very thin. For insecure girls, this is yet another criterion that can make or break them socially. Being in the cafeteria aggravates whatever inner battles they have about eating. Knowing that their classmates or friends are watching them magnifies their discomfort. Everything girls put in their mouths becomes public knowledge.

Teens are well aware of friends who sit and pick at grapes or eat only two carrot sticks at a time. They know who pushes food around on her plate and who gorges on bagels and candy bars, only to visit the restroom afterward. Often girls wonder if the problem is serious and whether their friends are getting the help they need. Some agonize over whether to reveal their concerns to teachers or guidance counselors.

But girls who struggle with eating also affect their peers, often intensifying their friends' self-consciousness. Witnesses to disordered eating, claims Pamela, a high school junior, "are more aware of what they're putting in their own mouths, how their jeans fit, their degree of thinness compared to their friends."

As usual, girls on both ends of the spectrum feel most pressured. While, as Marcie said, fat girls are shunned, thin girls incite envy and accusation. "I am five feet one and I weigh about ninety-five pounds. I'm not anorexic or bulimic," writes one *Girls' Life* reader. "I am simply a very petite person. I have hopes of being a model or actress, but if I get famous, I don't want the kind of coverage that criticizes naturally thin models and celebrities all the time."

More socially confident teens are better able to cope. "It's all about accepting yourself," says Kate, who is one of only a few girls helping herself to bagels and cream cheese one morning in our first-period focus group. "My friends are all into dieting. They get mad at me because I'm eating in front of them," she continues. "But I have a fast metabolism and I just don't care how I look. They won't eat, and I'll eat whatever I want." It is clear that Kate is too secure to worry about alienating her friends.

Focus on Appearance. Although everyone knows that many teen girls become preoccupied with their looks, the extent of their insecurity often remains hidden. This is something the girls in my high school focus group can agree upon. One morning, they are eager to confide their own personal "horror stories" about how they looked in middle school. It sounds like the giddy self-disclosures that occur in the wee hours of a sleepover.

All these girls recall feeling self-conscious and ashamed of looking not quite right. As I listen to them, the irony hits me. Every teen, intent upon trying to fit in, was so consumed by her own self-doubt that she didn't know that other girls felt exactly the same way. Unable to commiserate with and comfort each other, they *all* felt alone.

Lindsey, one of the more outgoing in this group, is the first to describe her trials. "I was the ugliest back then. Remember, I had these bangs? I used to roll them with a round brush and they were like this:" She makes a dramatic, swooping gesture. "I would blow-dry it, and it was thick, a big ball of hair. I had braces too; I was really cute!" she says sarcastically. The other girls giggle with her, clearly enjoying the diversion.

"Well, I decided to grow out my bangs in sixth grade," says Kyle. "I used to pull my hair back and gel it really tightly. Sometimes I put too much gel in, and it would flake. It was so traumatic!" She says this with urgency, as if it had happened yesterday.

"For me," Sterling adds, "it was my clothes. My friends never said to me, 'That is an ugly shirt.' It was more what I would be saying to myself, 'Wow, I just got this shirt, but is it as nice as hers? Maybe it is really ugly and I shouldn't have bought it.'"

Girls most often look to their appearance as a source of esteem when they doubt they can keep up with rising academic demands. All teens are vulnerable; no matter how smart they are, they reach a point when they can no longer coast. Unless they adapt and develop new skills, they can't maintain good grades. Amy claims she doesn't care about her poor report card, but deep down, she fears losing her teachers' respect.

Turning to her appearance, Amy studies what other kids wear, trying to figure out why the most popular girls seem to be able to throw things together that look cool, whereas she is accused of being mismatched. She begs her mother to take her to the trendiest stores, where she knows these popular girls shop, but she only succeeds in further riling her mother about succumbing to peer pressure.

Obsessing about appearance also takes its toll. Research shows that women's discomfort about body size and shape drains their mental energy and impedes their academic performance. Psychologists at the University of Michigan asked college students to put on either sweaters or swimsuits and complete tests while eating candy bars alone in dressing rooms. Men reported feeling silly, but women felt ashamed. And while women generally scored lower than men on math tests, when they wore swimsuits—and presumably felt more self-conscious—the gap widened. It is all too easy to understand how issues of appearance can affect performance in the classroom.

HELPING INSECURE GIRLS

The first step for parents intent upon helping insecure daughters is to better understand and empathize with their distress. This goes a long way toward defusing conflict and halting downward spirals before they become crises. Girls feel immediate relief from shame and far more supported. In Amy's case, learning about her parents' isolation when they were teens is comforting because it helps her to put their attitudes in perspective. Although her parents are set in their ways, they try to be open to hearing what can help their daughter. These strategies can encourage teens to gain much-needed acceptance:

▶ Modify Parental Involvement

Through counseling, Amy's parents learn that many of their efforts are actually unhelpful. For example, admonishing their daughter to be less social is insensitive; she is desperate for a friend. Although they are trying to comfort her when they tell her that the girls who rebuff her "aren't good enough for you," they stop when they realize it is more hurtful. Giving Amy specific suggestions, such as "Why don't you invite over so-and-so?" only angers and insults her. Girls generally scoff at these offered panaceas, as well as their parents' audacity in thinking they know best.

Along with encouraging them to step back in these ways, I suggest that Amy's parents explore other avenues of help. They make an appointment with their daughter's guidance counselor, who offers several resources. At her mother's request, the guidance counselor agrees to meet with Amy during her free periods to coach her on making new friends, including how to approach girls who are receptive and start conversations. She also invites Amy to join the newly forming lunch bunch, a social skills group specifically for middle school girls.

► Encourage Mainstream Behavior

Although Amy's parents want to protect her from destructive peer pressure, I help them to appreciate the benefit of their daughter's becoming more attuned to popular culture. They come to understand that shared experiences help her to join in and feel included in classmates' conversations. Many of our sessions address how Amy's parents can maintain their values while also relaxing some of their strictest rules. For example, they agree to allow her to listen to certain nonclassical CDs. Her mother also watches a teen TV show with her to give Amy something to talk about at school.

It is harder for Amy's mother to accept her desire to blend in with her peers, even to look cool. Unlike some women, she is indifferent to her own appearance. Also, she finds the attire of middle school students genuinely appalling. So whenever Amy asks to have a specific pair of sneakers or jeans, her mother gets upset and reminds her of the importance of staying true to herself. Amy's mother seems comforted by my stories of other girls I know who struggle with this same issue.

Corey, another mother of a middle schooler, is concerned that her daughter is indifferent to her appearance. While darkening body hair embarrasses her friends, Marie seems unaware of her "unibrow" and hairy legs. Corey admires her daughter's confidence and does not want to make her self-conscious, but to spare Marie from being teased as "the weird girl," she tactfully offers to help her wax or use a depilatory.

Mothers who are less knowledgeable about cultural trends or who are uneasy handling these issues can turn to others. Perhaps aunts, older sisters, or even family friends can lend girls a hand with picking out clothing or introductions to mainstream styles. Sometimes all it takes to boost girls' social confidence and gain acceptance is a new outfit or haircut that helps them to feel attractive and conform to the current look.

► Enlist Teachers' Assistance

Teachers can be godsends to insecure students. If you make them aware that your daughter is feeling isolated, they may be able to make thoughtful assignments for homework buddies, study or lab partners, and project groups. In other words, they can facilitate your daughter's interaction with classmates who are similar to her and most likely to work cooperatively with her. Teachers can also monitor the progress of the group to ensure that one student is neither controlling the others nor doing all the work, which are pet peeves among many girls in middle school and high school.

If you are comfortable with your daughter's teachers, you might make them aware that she needs support to avoid her becoming disenfranchised. If they know that she fears being singled out and embarrassed, they may be more sensitive to how they handle issues such as answering questions and handing back grades. If they know she responds well to praise, they might be more inclined to mention what she is doing right. If her teachers know that she feels intimidated, they might monitor the level of verbal aggression and competition in the classroom. Above all, you might ask them to suggest what your daughter might do to be more accepted.

► Facilitate Potential Friendships

Many girls who lack social ties within school are able to make friends more easily through outside activities. You might encourage your daughter to attend summer camp and church- or synagogue-sponsored events where she can meet kids with similar backgrounds and beliefs. Many find volunteer work satisfying, such as building houses for Habitat for Humanity. Others join theater groups or clubs that tend to be more tolerant of diversity. You can best help by offering to drive your daughter and potential friends when they are younger, and opening your home (stocked with appealing refreshments, of course) to older kids who want to hang out.

Outside of school, insecure girls are able to shed old reputations and start fresh away from the judgmental eyes of their classmates. Shared activities and teamwork also give girls a basis for discussion. (Please note, however, that team sports are often too intimidating because of their intense competition. Girls are afraid of not coming through or making mistakes that would incur the wrath of their teammates.)

If your daughter is in middle school, she may be comforted by the knowledge that girls usually find it easier to make friends and feel included in high school. Teens describe their peers as generally kinder and more accepting. Also, high schools tend to be larger, offering the chance to meet more kids and join a greater number of activities. As girls become more mobile, they can expand their activities outside of school and therefore widen their social network. For example, I know girls who take up swing dancing, life drawing, or fashion design, or become drummers or lead singers in garage bands.

Even one friendly acquaintance makes all the difference. After I have been working with Amy and her family for a while, she writes a poem for the school's literary journal. This helps her to get to know the editor, a kind eighth grader who takes an interest in her. Amy sits with Noelle at lunch one day to talk about an upcoming issue. Soon after, she goes to a high school basketball game with Noelle and her friends. "School isn't so bad now," Amy tells me hopefully.

Feeling understood comforts insecure girls. The right kind of adult encouragement reduces their anxiety and instills better social skills. As soon as a teen makes a new friend or feels included in a group, her whole outlook improves and she is that much better able to succeed in all areas of her life.

CHAPTER 7

Burning Too Bright: Perfectionistic Girls

Teenage girls are notorious experts at hiding pain, but one stressed-out group especially escapes notice: perfectionists. This is because they usually do so well. These girls are generally conscientious, hardworking high achievers. Because they take initiative, hold themselves to high standards, and persevere until they reach their goals, their parents don't have to stay on top of them. Their accomplishments delight their teachers. In fact, these girls are often held up as role models for their fellow students.

Perfectionists usually shine in their extracurricular activities, too, making their mark in sports, the arts, community service, and student government. Yet even this is not enough. These girls strive for perfection in their appearance and social connections as well. They are perpetually polite, cheerful, and helpful. They try to have the ideal body and to be the perfect student, friend, sister, girlfriend, and daughter.

You might be wondering what could be the problem with being—or raising—such a teen. In fact, if this is not your daughter's style, you might even be thinking it would be great if she were *more* like this. After all, perfectionists seem to have everything under control. They are efficient, competent, and independent. Whatever the job, they get it done well and hardly ever ask for help.

But be careful what you wish for. While many perfectionistic girls function well, they are at risk for trouble when things go wrong. The price of their compulsion for perfection is an even greater vulnerability to the destructive consequences of stress.

Perfectionistic teens mercilessly drive themselves to achieve their goals. As demonstrated by the stories that follow, for some girls this leads to procrastination, incomplete work, and, ultimately, a drop-off in performance. Others who are desperate to succeed resort to cutthroat behavior or cheating. Still others burn out. If they fail to reach their goals or experience more stress than they can handle, these girls are also prone to developing mental and physical illnesses. In their research, psychologists Paul Hewitt and Gordon Flett have found a correlation between perfectionism and anxiety, depression, eating disorders, and suicidal behavior.

It is hard for parents and teachers to know when girls are headed for crises; perfectionists not only do well, but they also create perfect façades of invincibility. So when do diligence and conscientiousness cross the line into perfectionism?

For example, should mothers and fathers commend the daughter who studies until two A.M. for her motivation and work ethic, or worry that she is overdoing it? Should teachers let the student who is distraught over a B plus do extra credit to raise her grade, or refer her for counseling? Should parents proudly support the daughter who runs for office in every student organization, or caution her to ease up and limit her obligations?

Unfortunately, it is only when girls develop obvious symptoms of distress that adults look back and see signs of unhealthy perfectionism in work habits that used to seem so admirable. The tip-off, in fact, may be that these girls seem to be doing *too* well—and doing too much. Two teens I saw in my practice illustrate the personality characteristics and underlying beliefs of perfectionistic girls, as well as the potential dangers of this pattern of behavior.

CELIA

In early fall, I get a call from Celia's mother, Marcella. She assures me that her daughter is a terrific girl, a straight-A eighth grader who has never given her parents any trouble. They are calling because of a medical problem. After many doctor visits and dreadful tests, Celia has just been diagnosed with a severe case of irritable bowel syndrome (IBS), a painful intestinal disorder that is thought to be stress related. Along with prescribing medication, her pediatrician recommended therapy to teach her better coping skills.

Since September, Celia has been awakening with stomach cramps and bouts of diarrhea that prevent her from getting to school until second or third period; on bad days, she can't leave her house. Whereas other girls might be thrilled by such an excuse to stay home, Celia is distraught. The thought of making up work overwhelms her. And she is afraid to miss a single minute of class because she believes no one takes notes as thoroughly as she does.

Marcella and David are shocked by their daughter's problem. They tell me that Celia has always been their relatively "easy" child, far less challenging than her older sister. Although she is a competitive figure skater, plays soccer, takes piano lessons, and does community service, she still manages to excel in school. "There is, though, one thing about Celia," Marcella admits. "She's always a little emotional." When I ask what that means, she says, "Sometimes little things set her off and she has meltdowns, like refusing to get out of the car and go to her piano lesson."

Alarmed by their daughter's illness, Marcella and her husband are eager for me to see her. But she warns me that Celia is not enthusiastic about going to a therapist. Like most perfectionistic girls, she is determined to be the best in everything. Going to therapy is tantamount to admitting that there is something wrong with her. With much coaxing, however, Celia agrees to meet with me just once.

It is a brisk November day when I first see Celia, a soft-spoken girl with stylishly cut short hair and intense dark eyes. She is in a great mood, she says, because of the report card she just got. I look at her expectantly, but she glances at her hands, which are folded neatly in her lap, to hide her grin. Celia is bursting to tell me her grades, but she is used to restraint. She doesn't want to seem boastful. I have to ask directly before she tells me, "straight A plusses." When I ask about her classes, however, her recitation sounds robotic:

> *Most of them are kind of boring. I'm in mostly honors classes—that's one year ahead—and the only accelerated— that's two years ahead—math class in my school for eighth grade. It's geometry, which is normally taken in tenth grade. My favorite subject is science. But my teacher is pretty bad and she's the same teacher I have for math.*

What is so bad about this teacher? I wonder. Celia seems frantic as she tells me: "She doesn't ever prepare us for tests. She goes over stuff at the end of class and tells us it won't be on the test, and then it is. Or there'll be other stuff she doesn't go over that we've never seen before." Clearly, this teacher's style panics her.

Many girls in middle school and even high school get angry when their teachers test them on material they haven't covered. Feeling unprepared makes them anxious, so they do poorly. But since Celia's grades are nearly perfect, I ask her how she thinks this teacher is affecting her performance. This is when I hear about her extraordinarily high standards for success—as well as the toll they are taking on her.

"When I get a bad teacher, I worry about if I'm going to be

ahead of everybody else, or with the rest of the class, or be way be-hind," Celia says, twirling the strings of her sweat pants. "I like be-ing up there, the best." Asked how she defines the best, she continues: "I think A's ranging from 90 to 95 percent are okay, but I honestly feel pressure to get at least 97 percent or better on most everything, even though I know colleges don't look at middle school grades." For Celia, perfect grades are the sine qua non.

She brings this same competitive edge to sports. As she tells me, "I like to do the best I can in everything, not just in school." A tal-ented athlete, she juggles practices and games for premier soccer teams with figure skating competitions. How can she possibly do all this? "Oh," she begins, slowly revealing her pain: "I guess stress is a problem for me. I'm a worrier. Before my competitions, I feel really sick. Sometimes I get these awful cramps. Like if I get a B plus on something, I have, like, a breakdown."

Celia agrees to come back, probably because at last she feels un-derstood. She has been going about her business as if nothing both-ers her. Until her body betrayed her, her parents and teachers had no idea of her distress. But in my conversations with Celia during the next few weeks, I hear about more destructive beliefs that typi-cally drive the efforts of perfectionistic girls. "I always have to meet everyone's expectations and be strong. If I don't, I feel that I failed," she sighs. "But it's actually hard to make everyone happy."

Therapy gives perfectionistic teens a safe place to sort out their values and priorities. They develop a clearer picture of who they are, where their strengths lie, and what really gratifies them. When they gradually realize that they can make mistakes and survive, girls come to terms with their flaws. They learn that others don't usually hold them to the lofty standards they have for themselves. Little by little, girls begin to cope better. And when they do, they become more enthusiastic about learning.

Kiera, a resilient *Girls' Life* reader who enjoys the support of her parents and teachers, expresses this tolerant attitude:

*Nobody is perfect. We are all human beings who make mis-
takes. My parents are really supportive of me, which I love.
My dad says if you tried your hardest, that's what counts. We
all get a bad grade every now and then, but you build off of it.
You fix your mistakes. The purpose of school is to learn. I have
three favorite teachers to always give me great advice. I try to
be the best that I can possibly be, and my best is enough.*

BIANCA

Bianca's story also demonstrates how easy it is to miss signs of an
impending crisis. A tenth grader, Bianca has been a good but not
stellar student, is well liked by all, and is involved in her school.
She has never before alarmed her parents or teachers. That is, until she is caught cheating on an English exam. When told she will
have to go before her high school's disciplinary committee, Bianca
feels devastated and humiliated. As she walks to gym with her
friends, she casually mentions that her family would be better off
without her. Her friends tell her guidance counselor, who notifies
her parents. Then they call me.

Naturally, they are shocked and distraught. So are Bianca's
teachers: She is the last student they would suspect of cheating.
She obeys rules and always wants to do the right thing. The only
trouble is that she keeps turning in her English assignments late—
or not at all. This makes no sense to them. Bianca is a gifted creative writer. In eighth grade she won fifty dollars for first place in a
short story contest. She cares about her grades, so why wouldn't
she get her work in on time to avoid losing points?

Bianca is a tall, slender teen whose olive skin and large, dark
eyes give her an exotic appearance. Clearly worried about coming
in to see me, the first thing she says is that her comment to her
friends was blown out of proportion. "I didn't mean I would kill

myself. I would never do that. I could never do that. It's just that sometimes it's hard to be as great as I want to be. I can't seem to do everything as well as I should," she admits. "Sometimes I feel like giving up."

The root of this problem, her hidden perfectionism, is soon made clear. Bianca's obsession about getting things exactly right is sabotaging her writing. "I really love English, especially analyzing stories. But I can't do my writing assignments," she tells me, "because I want people to be impressed with me and admire my work." Her aim is not just to get good grades; Bianca wants to astonish her teachers. "To write well," she explains, "I have to feel what I'm writing. So I postpone writing until I think I can get an impressive result. I look for the wow."

With this goal, it is little surprise that she finds writing torturous. Thinking that every sentence will be evaluated as the final word on her talent, she wrestles with herself before committing each syllable to paper. Because of her writer's block, all of her parents' coaxing and lecturing is for naught. Procrastination enables Bianca to put off the possibility of writing something inferior—and therefore, in her mind, failing.

If inspiration doesn't come, Bianca writes nothing. Determined to protect her reputation as a smart and talented writer, she would rather get a zero than turn in something mediocre. "I'd rather keep this image than fail to meet my teacher's standards. If you get a bad grade, it's stuck with you forever," she says. "That's worse than just points off for handing in something late." Fear of imperfection paralyzes her.

Although Bianca is mortified about plagiarizing her Shakespeare exam, her motive was clear: She was desperate for the wow. Perfectionists live in fear of not being the best. Because this threatens their core identity, girls have been known to become overly competitive and even ruthless. Teens sabotage their classmates' achievement by removing reference materials from libraries. They plagiarize people's work, copy from classmates, rip out pages from resource materials, and steal tests.

Cheating is far more common than many adults would imagine. When girls are asked what they would change to make their school experience better, a number say, "Less cheating." A sophomore told me, "Kids in high school are crazy. If you get all A's, a lot of people think you're perfect and like to copy from you. My friend still has people who cheat off her and she doesn't like to say no. I do. It's wrong and I won't let them."

In this anxiety-ridden culture, it should be no surprise that cheating is on the rise among students. Rutgers University management professor Donald McCabe found that more than half of the more than four thousand high school students he surveyed had taken sentences and paragraphs from Web sites, and 15 percent had copied entire papers. In a more recent survey of sixteen thousand undergraduate students, 38 percent admitted to Internet cheating, up from 10 percent in 2000. Remarkably, 44 percent of students said it was no big deal.

Teens desperate to succeed may also be more inclined to cheat today because they are getting the message that it is condoned. A recent large-scale study of middle and high schools found that although 40 percent give mandatory out-of-school suspensions the first time students are caught smoking, only 4 percent of schools have such a policy for first-time cheating offenses.

Ironically, it is the highest achievers who usually get away with cheating and other unethical behaviors. Parents and teachers are deceived because intellectual superiority is often equated with moral superiority. This struck me when I received a call from a panicked woman whose daughter, a freshman, wanted to come home from boarding school after pornographic pictures of her had been posted on the Internet and circulated among her schoolmates. As she related the story, this mother kept repeating, "But Molly is a straight-A student!" She seemed shocked that her daughter's academic achievement hadn't inoculated her against poor judgment—or its consequences.

Bianca's cheating ordeal uncovers another symptom of her perfectionism: Her impatience with uncertainty or perceived stupidity results in run-ins with her classmates. Although she is aware that her bossiness and harsh judgments alienate her peers, her need for perfection is too compelling; she can't help herself: "It's so frustrating when kids are clueless about what's going on. Or they say they'll do something and either they don't, or they do it so badly. I hate when my teachers give us group projects. I'm not going to get a bad grade just because of them."

Although perfectionistic teens are usually reliable and hard-working, they often lack the tolerance, patience, and flexibility that are necessary for effective teamwork. They can't accept that their friends, teachers, and parents aren't perfect either.

THE TOLL OF PERFECTIONISM

How can parents and teachers become more alert to signs that trouble may be brewing? First, it helps to be clear on the difference between the pursuit of excellence, which can be healthy, and perfectionism, which is not.

In her book *Perfectionism*, which is geared for young people, psychologist Miriam Adderholdt-Elliott describes ambitious students as having high standards for achievement, preparing effectively, taking tests with confidence, and feeling good about how they perform. They are able to try new things, accept positive feedback with pride, and learn from their mistakes. Above all, they enjoy learning. In contrast, although perfectionists exhibit relentless determination, their anxiety about their performance and self-defeating beliefs prevent them from taking intellectual risks and solving problems well.

Relentless Determination

Perfectionistic girls are defined by extraordinarily high goals combined with an absolute intolerance for falling short. Bianca is unapologetic about her ambition: "The most important thing is being right. I feel like I need to be correct in whatever situation I'm in. I know it's unrealistic, but I strive hard. I can't mess up."

When driven girls believe their goals are threatened, they redouble their efforts to succeed. Parents don't usually recognize such relentlessness as unhealthy. Until Celia becomes ill, for example, her studiousness pleases her parents. They can relate. Maybe if they themselves were lower-keyed, their daughter's intensity would set off a warning bell. But as it is, they don't see her distress. Because her meltdowns wax and wane, her parents are misled into thinking there is no real problem.

Test-Taking Anxiety

Although many teen girls occasionally become anxious about taking tests, perfectionists experience this more commonly and severely. As I get to know Celia, she reveals, "I usually get so worried when I have tests coming up. Like this week I had a big math test on Wednesday, and Tuesday night I cried for an hour. Even though I studied, I was afraid I'd see something I didn't know on the test and freak out." For a girl with IBS, getting worked up is ill advised. Sure enough, by Wednesday morning Celia's stomach is in knots and she has to wait until her cramps subside to go to school.

Because perfectionists usually bottle up their apprehension, it is not uncommon for them to develop physical symptoms such as headaches, migraines, stomachaches, ulcers, and sleep problems—

or for their existing medical problems to worsen. Girls may have trouble waking up and getting to school on time whenever they anticipate a nerve-racking test or oral report. On a stressful morning, what parents may see is a daughter rushing around and skipping breakfast, more silent than usual, or sniping at her sibling.

If this is chronic, parents and teachers may have to help girls get to the root of their anxiety. Is the desire for perfection freezing them? Are girls as well prepared as they think they are? Or do they need to meet with their teachers for extra help or study sessions? Some girls benefit from reviewing tests to familiarize themselves with new or challenging formats. Others find it a relief to study with friends. A few need relaxation techniques, which are described later in this chapter.

Quianna, a member of one of my focus groups, knows how to coach herself before tests: "I don't let myself get pressured. For me, well, I'm not going to worry because if I don't worry, I do better. I go into every test calm, like it's going to be nothing. I won't get worked up. I figure if I know it, I know it. If not, it's only a test."

Avoidance of Risk

When girls realize they can't always be right, they are more resilient to life's hurdles. When they encounter setbacks, they cope by focusing on the positive: What can I learn from this? What can I do to improve? This outlook results in powerful learning opportunities. As Keith Cowie, a school psychologist, has said, "In general, a guarantee of 100 percent success may take away an opportunity to grow. Zero failing can be very limiting."

Because they fear feeling lost or humiliated, however, perfectionistic girls avoid paths that are not well marked. This inhibits them from experimenting, trying out ideas, and making discoveries. They also don't get to test out their skills or courage. As Celia describes, "I can't stand when I'm not positive of something." If she thinks she doesn't understand, she leaves questions blank rather than guessing. That way, she can't be wrong. Of course, she can't be right either.

The director of an independent school spoke of what can happen to girls who can't admit to feeling confused:

> *One of the concerns we always have is that girls who are afraid to take academic risks appear to understand concepts, but they don't. And then we don't have a chance to correct it. Later, you find they're missing critical things. They don't believe it's okay to make a mistake and not have it come out right. They don't see it that way, and their parents don't see it that way.*

Rigid Problem Solving

Ironically, the relentless determination of perfectionism can backfire. Anxiety interferes with clear thinking and productivity like nothing else. When teenage girls are apprehensive, they tend to latch onto the first solution they encounter. Or they become indecisive or wishy-washy, essentially becoming stuck. Other girls endlessly second-guess themselves. They wear out their erasers changing their answers and redoing items they think they can improve. This, of course, only wastes time and exacerbates stress.

Because of Bianca's difficulty getting her work done and handing it in on time, her parents worry that she might have a learning disability. They ask me to test her. The story she tells in response to the first card of the Thematic Apperception Test, the boy with the violin, portrays the paralyzing effects of obsessive self-doubt and fears of imperfection:

There's a boy, and he looks pretty sad. He's looking at a violin, trying to think of what to play. There's a piece of paper under him. Maybe he'll write his music on it. He's thinking hard. He's thinking about if he has a recital coming up, if he can really do it. If he can really play the piece without making a mistake. If he's really ready.

Given such ruminations, it is no wonder Bianca has trouble breaking down her assignments and getting started. When her parents see her staring into space at her desk, they think she is wasting time. But she says, "If I have a big assignment or project, it's a lot of work. Sometimes I get so frustrated, I can't do anything. It's all so big." What she is expressing is feeling overwhelmed, a word that describes many stressed-out teens, but especially epitomizes perfectionists.

Self-defeating Beliefs

Parents and teachers who hear—or sense—any of these self-defeating attitudes in highly achieving girls should suspect tendencies toward perfectionism:

"I'm Upset with Myself." Perfectionists can't let go of their perceived mistakes. Although a year has passed, Bianca still talks about not being selected for honors biology. She still ponders where she went wrong and what she should have done differently. "I think it was because of my third-quarter science grade in eighth grade," she speculates. "Maybe I should've studied more. I had gotten a pretty big part in the play that year, one of the leads, and I was at practice every day for three hours. I should've realized. If I hadn't . . ." On and on, she admonishes herself.

Celia too engages in self-defeating thought processes. And because she knows she *shouldn't* be thinking this way, she no sooner tells me something than she takes it back: "Well, I beat myself up—well, not literally—when I get Bs. I guess I kind of get—well, not angry at myself, but maybe—I don't get angry at myself, but I guess I stress. I worry. I feel like I've kind of let myself down."

Apparently, this attitude is not at all uncommon. When young teen readers of *Girls' Life* magazine were asked about the pressures they experience to do well in school, they sent a deluge of e-mails describing thoughts and behaviors that exemplify perfectionism:

+ "I am a straight-A student, yet I feel dissatisfied with myself."
+ "I am in advanced classes. I feel like I always have to make A's, and if I don't, then I call myself dumb."
+ "I'll stay up all night trying to think of ways to be better. I can spend up to two hours trying to look pretty. I've had thoughts of dieting and being anorexic."
+ "I feel nothing but pressure in school. Teachers and parents have such high expectations that it is hard to live up to. But the person I feel the most pressure from is myself. If I don't do well, I get upset and depressed."
+ "School is very important to me. I always do all of my work. If I don't get an A on everything, I start to cry and think that the world is over."

Resilient girls, on the other hand, can accept their shortcomings—and even find humor in them. Karla, a member of my focus groups, trips as she sits down at the table one morning, laughs out loud, and announces dramatically, "And . . . for my grand entrance!" A teacher told me about another buoyant girl: "Leann is a hopeless athlete, but she thinks it's hilarious. She can make mistakes and not be good at something. That makes her so much stronger than girls who can't do that."

"I Can Be Better!" When I ask teen girls about the one thing they would change to make their school experience better, I expect to hear about different classes, more helpful teachers, or better facilities. And I do hear these requests. But I am surprised by the number of teens who respond with specifics about what they would change (read *improve*) about themselves. These goals are largely unrealistic:

+ "I would know everything in the world."
+ "I would be the smartest."
+ "I would get nothing less than 100 percent on everything."
+ "I would have a perfect report card every time."
+ "I would have an A-plus-plus average."

A need to be the absolute best makes perfectionistic girls hypersensitive to criticism. As with square pegs, their parents and teachers often complain that they "can't say a word" or "have to walk on eggs" to avoid inciting outbursts. When girls crave approval and overreact to even gentle suggestions or constructive criticism, it is a clue that their self-esteem may be brittle.

Perfectionists have trouble grasping the principle that no one can be perfect. No matter how terrific they are, there will always be someone who is smarter, prettier, or more popular. No matter how hard they work, there will always be someone who is more creative, gets more playing time, or earns higher SAT scores. Unless they come to terms with this reality, learning of others' successes will always diminish their own accomplishments, deflating their gratification and pride in a heartbeat.

"It's Never Enough!" Perfectionists rarely savor their accomplishments. They can't reward themselves for reaching a goal because they are already focusing on the next one. There is always

something more extraordinary to be achieved. When Celia gets the only A in her class on a science test, she says, "I was happy for about a minute. Then I started worrying about the final, and whether I would be able to do that again." With every achievement, in fact, perfectionists set the bar even higher. The thinking goes, "If I can reach this goal, it must not be so impressive. I should do even better next time."

In the same way, perfectionistic girls often believe that the better they do, the more their parents and teachers expect of them. Once they demonstrate how capable they are, they perceive even more intense pressure. Landra, for example, writes in an e-mail, "If you are smart, your parents can expect that all the time." Marissa says:

> I do really well in school. Most people would think that I am lucky, and that they would want to be me. Actually, you probably wouldn't. Because of how well I usually do, my parents' standards for me are very high. They expect me to get straight A's, and if I get even a B plus they ask why that happened. For anyone else, a B plus would be great, but not for me. It puts a lot of pressure on me. Everyone expects so much from me. So it's not always perfect to be perfect.

The girls in my focus groups report similar experiences.

"I feel so bad when I get a bad grade, I know my parents are going to kill me," says Allison.

"Yeah, if you got a 95, they go, 'Why not a 98?'" agrees Monica.

Jenny is smiling and nodding. "Or, how about, 'You got a 95? What happened to those five other points?'" she adds.

"It's not just parents," says Amy. "Since my teachers know I can do really well in school, they act all surprised when I make mistakes."

With their sensitivity to criticism, perfectionists tend to take their parents' and teachers' words literally. Casual comments, especially those said in jest or tinged with irony, tend to be interpreted in the severest possible way—that is, much like these teens speak to themselves. With this mind-set, girls may not be able to distinguish between encouragement and pressure to perform. For example, a supportive comment such as "I have a lot of confidence in you. I know you can do this!" can all too easily be heard as "I expect you to do this; don't disappoint me!"

"I Have No Idea What I Want." Many perfectionists achieve for the wrong reasons. Gifted girls like Celia are often compelled to excel in every area simply because they can. Bianca's fixed desire to be spectacular undermines her writing. Other girls are intent upon achieving to avoid thinking about disconcerting adolescent issues, such as figuring out who they are, who they want to be, and what they want from life. With empty goals, however, teens progressively become estranged from what truly excites them and lose their joy in achievement.

When perfectionistic girls complain of being bored, they are often expressing this detachment from their inner motivation. It is not that they need more stimulation or challenge; they have to reconnect with their feelings about what they like and dislike. In April, when Celia has to choose her classes for high school, she doesn't consider what interests her, how to make her schedule manageable, or how much academic pressure is right for her. Instead, she asks, "How many honors classes do colleges want? They'll see them on my transcript, right? Don't you get extra points added to your GPA for honors classes?"

In therapy, however, she is encouraged to explore her real desires. At first, her answer is always, "I don't know. I never thought about that." When Celia considers quitting figure skating to avoid panicking before competitions, she tells me, "I wish my parents would say it's okay. But they keep telling me I have talent, and I've put so much into this already. They say I have to work on getting over the stress, but I don't know if it's worth it." Actually, this dilemma is a sign of progress. As her inner voice tries to alert her to what really matters, she is starting to pay closer attention.

"If I Can't Be Best, I Can't Be Anything!" As perfectionists look toward ever-larger goals, they dread slipping up and losing their status. They are plagued by shame, guilt, and embarrassment over mistakes and failures that others might dismiss as trivial. Like gerbils running on wheels, these stressed-out girls soon exhaust themselves and feel as though they can never get anywhere. With their characteristic black-or-white thinking, they feel like abject failures if they can't be perfect. When the pain of their imperfections seems intolerable and they doubt ever feeling better, a few perfectionists even become self-destructive.

When I ask to read one of Bianca's short stories, I meet a fictional character, an aspiring young artist who "wishes to be known as the greatest artist that ever lived." She is plagued by doubts about how her work will be received. When "the manager of the art gallery despised her paintings and claimed she had no talent at all, the artist was completely crushed, with nowhere to turn and nurse her broken pride. She took her own life that night." The unmistakable moral of Bianca's story is "If you don't achieve your goals, you're not perfect—and then life is not worth living."

According to the American Association of Suicidology, youth suicides are on the rise. Since 1980, the suicide rate has increased 99 percent among ten- to fourteen-year-olds and 11 percent in the fifteen- to nineteen-year-old age group. Among fifteen- to twenty-four-year olds, including college students, suicides have tripled. Approximately twelve young people kill themselves every day. Girls end their lives less often than boys, but make significantly more nonlethal attempts. Some of these gestures, with pills, for example, damage their health or accidentally kill them.

A study conducted at Pennsylvania State University may shed light on family dynamics affecting suicidal behavior among undergraduates. Consistent with the national average, researchers found that about 20 percent of college students reported thoughts of suicide. But when they looked into what led to actual attempts, they discovered factors that increase young women's risk of suicide.

The most at-risk female students had mothers who not only expected stellar academic performance, but also kept raising the bar, and fathers who conformed to their mothers' nonnegotiable standards. This group of young women proved far more vulnerable than young men to the harmful effects of their mothers' demands for perfection; their risk of attempted suicide was four times that of their male counterparts.

HELPING PERFECTIONISTIC GIRLS

► Counteract Self-defeating Attitudes

If you recognize signs of perfectionism in your daughter, you will undoubtedly try to head off a crisis before it develops. But even if self-defeating beliefs are entrenched, there is still much you can do. It is never too late to try to instill a healthy perspective about achievement. You might start with your daughter's daily schedule. Set limits on homework hours so that she doesn't burn the midnight lava lamp and study excessively. Make her choose her favorite activities rather than cram too much into her agenda.

When working with your daughter—whether sewing a costume, doing a science project, or fixing something around the house—model how to tolerate confusion, cope with frustration, and find answers patiently. Demonstrate that all feelings are okay; having "bad" emotions doesn't make her a bad person. In fact, give her permission to vent. Carlyn describes the benefits: "If I have a lot of work, or if I don't understand something, sometimes I just stop doing it. I take a break. Sometimes I do something else or else I just cry. It doesn't last more than twenty minutes. It's not that big of a deal."

► Deemphasize Achievements

To increase your daughter's resiliency, help her not to base her self-esteem on her wins, scores, or other external measures of achievement. Reiterate that she is not defined by her accomplishments—or lack thereof. Instead, emphasize the value of her personal qualities, such as her sense of humor, honesty, helpfulness, loyalty, warmth, integrity, playfulness, and so forth.

You might also examine whether you are inadvertently giving her harmful messages about perfection. How do you respond to less than ideal grades? Do you urge your daughter to try harder? Do you say nothing, perhaps leaving her to interpret your silence as evidence of your approval—or disapproval? Do you expect her to take honors classes if she is capable of doing so? Or do you ask instead why she wants to take AP bio? Does she love the subject or just think it will look good for college?

The most important message parents need to convey is that daughters are lovable despite their inevitable imperfections. Girls must be assured that their mothers and fathers care more about who they are than about what they accomplish. And they have to know in their heart of hearts that when they falter, their parents may be disappointed *for* them, but not *in* them.

► Monitor and Reduce Nervous Energy

There are limits to what you, as a parent, can do to counteract your daughter's perfectionism. Some girls have innate dispositions that predispose them to becoming highly focused, detail oriented, and exacting. This is part of their character; they do not stop being perfectionists just because their parents suggest they lighten up.

But it is also true that when mothers and fathers can monitor their own nervous energy, their daughters benefit immensely. One, the level of anxiety in the home is lower. Two, girls don't have to feel so responsible for worrying their parents. Three, parents who are more relaxed are more attuned to their daughters and less likely to push teens into areas for which they are neither well suited nor ready. Four, parents are less likely to believe—or to convey—that every achievement is the final word on whether their girls will be successful.

Recognizing that the family's hectic lifestyle is not working for Celia, her parents slow down for her. They change their work schedules in order to be around more after school, providing a silent but supportive presence as Celia does her homework. Rather than seeing skating in a black-or-white way, they model flexibility: They reduce her stress by reducing her practice schedule and limiting her to two competitions per year. Celia is greatly relieved.

► Encourage Better Coping Skills

Girls are empowered by learning relaxation techniques for reducing stress. Therapists often teach strategies such as guided imagery, muscle relaxation, and deep breathing. Some teens enjoy yoga; others listen to soothing relaxation tapes. Many girls I work with find positive self-coaching effective in blocking self-defeating worries. They tell themselves: "You can do this" or "You don't have to be perfect" or "Just stop it!"

When Bianca and her parents meet with staff at her school, the psychologist and teacher suggest a number of strategies to overcome writer's block, such as writing outlines and doodling or drawing pictures before expressing herself with words. After trying different techniques, Bianca decided she prefers to use brightly colored rather than stark white paper, which intimidates her. She also finds it useful to talk out her ideas before putting them down on paper.

Here are suggestions from the girls I surveyed for relieving tension. Your daughter might find some of these activities soothing when she feels stressed out:

+ "Bake cookies, clean out my closet, draw, brush the dog, or look at photo albums."
+ "Take a second with a person—or a box of chocolates."
+ "Talk on the phone with your friends."
+ "Go out and party. Go bowling and hang out."
+ "Be with people, like friends who unstress you."
+ "I take a bath or give myself a facial."
+ "I walk around the pond with my friend."
+ "Listen to relaxing music or tapes."
+ "I do breathing exercises, yoga, or meditation."
+ "I deal with stress by playing my violin."
+ "Go online."
+ "I watch an old movie or read *Marjorie Morningstar* again."
+ "I take a nap."
+ "I read a teen magazine."

► Correct Misconceptions

Although this has been discussed, it is so vital for perfectionistic girls that it bears repeating. It is crucial to reflect on whether your daughter thinks you expect her to achieve in overly specific ways. Could she be living her life according to a script that she senses has been written for her from birth—or even before? Emma describes her best friend: "Back in elementary school, Dorie would get upset when she got a 99. I'm not kidding. Her parents are perfectionists. They knew what she should be when she was in elementary school. They had a plan for all their kids. One of them was going to be doctor and go to medical school."

In therapy, when Celia's parents clarify their expectations, she learns that they are okay with her not being as fast paced or competitive as they are. She is surprised to find out that they don't imagine her having a high-powered career in finance.

If your daughter is driven to perfection, it behooves you to consider whether she is responding, even unconsciously, to your hopes and dreams for her. If so, this gives you a clear path toward alleviating at least some of her distress.

► Encourage Her to Learn from Mistakes

With perfectionistic girls, parents are tempted to jump in early to smooth things over. You might wish to protect your daughter from disappointments that set off upsets, outbursts, or meltdowns. But as the principal of a large suburban high school told me, "Greater involvement with what kids are doing is not necessarily good. Parents are overinvolved. It would be good if they can let go of these girls more and let them make mistakes—and get what they need to out of those mistakes."

This is sage advice. No matter how hard your daughter works or how much you try to orchestrate her success, at times she still won't get what she wants. Despite a good tryout, for example, she may not be chosen for a special orchestra, a premier sports team, or a lead in the school play. Chance factors may get in the way, circumstances may be outrageously unfair, or she may not get the break she needs.

Teens have to be able to cope with such setbacks. That is why it is crucial not to rescue them from every misstep. When you don't rush in to excuse late papers or request grade changes or ask for more playing time on the field, small doses of disappointment and frustration inoculate your daughter against becoming overwhelmed when the truer, bigger disasters inevitably occur.

In addition to telling your daughter about your own mistakes and calamities, educate her about the early failures of women who later became highly successful. For example, the children's author Judy Blume received countless rejection letters before selling seven million copies of her first fourteen books. Similarly, another beloved children's author, Beverly Cleary, tells in her memoir of getting a D in a college botany course. Lugging around her botany book along with a pamphlet called *How to Study*, she learned to do several repetitions during the day and review her work at bedtime. As a result, she got an A for the semester, saw the D expunged, and earned a B plus for the year. She writes in her memoir, "I had learned a lesson more valuable than botany."

As parents, we can't assume that our daughters already know these lessons. We have to be mindful of repeating them, over and over, to counteract the extraordinary pressure for achievement they get from this culture, from their peers, and especially from themselves. The cost of perfectionism is far too great a risk. We don't want our daughters to burn so brightly that they burn out.

CHAPTER 8

Minds Elsewhere: Distracted Girls

It is hard to imagine a teenage girl who is *not* distracted by the occasional personal or family problem. On any given day she might find it hard to concentrate on—or even care about—what she is supposed to be learning because she is hurt by a friend's behavior, upset about a heated argument, or worried about illness in the family. She might be decidedly unenthusiastic about running laps in outdoor track or completely forget to do her English homework because she is obsessing about her father losing his job and whether her family will have to move.

In response to distressing but short-term life events, girls naturally feel out of sorts, preoccupied, anxious, or depressed. Although these emotional states are draining and disruptive, they are usually transient. Once stressful situations pass or problems are resolved, teens feel recharged. They reengage in their everyday lives and approach their activities with renewed energy and focus.

But when problems persist, accumulate, or become pervasive, it is harder to cope, especially for girls who charactistically have trouble handling strong emotions. That is why teens who constantly clash with their parents and teachers, have significant family troubles, or struggle with emotional disorders are particularly at risk. So are girls who endure traumas and those who tend to ruminate. When girls are bogged down by their inner lives, they have much less mental energy for achievement, activities, interests, and other external pursuits. Many adults are more familiar, since the tragedies of September 11, 2001, with the devastating effects on concentration of perpetual tension and heightened sensitivity to emotion. As Nancy described, "My mind is always busy. I need a vacation from my head."

Not every teen who goes through hard times develops symptoms. Those who can tuck away their troubles are less encumbered. They go about their daily business, maintain their routines, and keep accomplishing. Some resourceful girls, in fact, find that focusing on their activities and goals actually alleviates their pain. Also, a good number of resilient teens are blessed with the ability to find people who can comfort them and provide the emotional support they need.

But it is a different story for more vulnerable girls. Dwelling on their troubles traps them inside their own heads, preventing them from remaining alert and in the present. Of course they can't pay attention; their minds are elsewhere. Prolonged preoccupation siphons their creativity and saps their zest for learning. Teachers and parents typically describe these distracted teens as spacey, not all there, daydreaming, disengaged, going through the motions, unfocused, and, of course, underachieving.

Yet the concerns that prey upon girls' minds often remain a mystery to adults. As you will see in the pages ahead, some problems are too subtle or invisible to detect until a crisis erupts. In other cases, mothers and fathers may know there is trouble in their daughters' lives but underestimate its impact. It is also hard for teachers to know when irascibility, poor focus, and out-of-character behavior are the norm for adolescents or a cause for alarm. Some distracted teens are, in fact, experiencing undiagnosed—and untreated—anxiety, depression, and attention disorders.

Teens are typically reticent, but they especially hide problems they consider confusing, weird, or embarrassing. When something is amiss within the family, they are often downright secretive. As a result, girls who are harboring unexpressed worries and preoccupations are usually seen as lazy or unmotivated, and as a result, they feel terribly misunderstood. For Torie, a freshman, the signs of an impending crisis were ignored.

TORIE

Unlike some girls who hit a wall as freshmen, Torie's slow, insidious academic decline during ninth grade does not scream for attention. She gets to class on time. Her work may not be top rated, but it is completed and handed in; there are no reports of missing assignments. Torie's teachers don't complain about her behavior. But still, her parents are concerned because they know she is bright and believe she could be doing much better. Although they have tried many ways to motivate her, nothing so far has done the trick. Torie's grades haven't improved and, if anything, her parents believe her attitude is even worse.

Years ago, parents seeing this pattern might have taken a wait-and-see approach, chalking up less than stellar grades to starting high school, being a teenager, or even being a slow starter. But with the level of nervous energy circulating today, Torie's parents are well aware of what is at stake, and worry that unless she turns things around, she will limit her opportunities for the future. Since they can't put their finger on the problem, they bring her to me for psychological testing. What they want to know is whether an attention or learning disorder could be getting in her way in school.

With her height, physical maturity, and bearing, Torie looks more like a senior than a freshman. She sports shoulder-length brown hair tucked behind her ears, a dusting of freckles, and a big smile. When I ask why she thinks she's being tested, her ambivalence about school is readily apparent: "I should be doing well, but I'm not that successful. My grades aren't really that good. Well, they're okay, but not really good. It doesn't matter that much."

When I ask Torie for her take on what is holding her back, she offers a veritable laundry list of possibilities. "Everybody thinks I would do good if I'd only try, but there's too much on my mind. I don't like school. I'm lazy about it. I daze out during class. I have trouble concentrating. I put answers down, but not as fully or the way they want you to. I just do it to get it done." She says all this so nonchalantly that I can see how her parents think she is apathetic. But Torie's distress is betrayed by bursts of nervous giggling, after which she looks at me blankly, momentarily distracted, and says apologetically, "Oh, I'm sorry. What did you say again?"

Torie feels blamed for not doing well in school. "My parents think I'm doing this on purpose. I'm not," she protests, "but I'm not going to do anything differently." This comment is tinged with anger that is hard to read. I wonder what is prompting Torie to dig in her heels this way. "They bring it up all the time," she continues, "you know, about the future. But it doesn't faze me. I'm supposed to be doing good, but I don't really care that much. I just like coming in and seeing my friends every day. If I don't like what we're learning about, I don't really try. I know it's bad." Unlike other girls, who seem to fade away in telling their stories, Torie refuses to become invisible.

Distracting Thoughts and Feelings

Rather quickly I learn that Torie's feelings intrude upon her when she is supposed to be paying attention: "When I'm not preoccupied, I can keep my mind on things most of the time, but I'm always a stress ball. I keep everything inside. It's a feeling in my head.

All the things going around in my head make it hard for me to think. So then I get in bad moods, and I get headaches a lot." When Torie tells her parents that reading books in English bores her, they don't recognize her "boredom" as a reflection of the more urgent need to manage her disturbing thoughts and feelings.

Like other teens who become distracted by stressful events, she tends to be a worrier. Torie is quick to say she obsesses and can't let things go. This is compounded by her family's practice of sweeping uncomfortable feelings under the rug. Because she has nowhere else to process her experiences and emotions, in class she dwells on whatever happened at breakfast or the night before. Torie tells me:

> When other things are on my mind, it's like school is extra. I don't concentrate on what my teacher is saying, especially if they go on and on. My mind is like—when I read, my mind wanders, especially if I'm in a fight with someone. I can't stop thinking about it and I can't understand the stories. I read every page five times. It's like, "What did I just read?"

She is also sensitive to external noise. When taking a test, "people chewing gum, whispering, bouncing their leg, or tapping drives me crazy."

Psychoeducational testing confirms that Torie is indeed a bright girl with strong academic skills; there is no learning or attention disorder that can account for her lackluster grades or apparent lack of motivation. Instead, emotional issues seem to be holding her back. It is not until Torie meets with me in therapy, however, that the real story behind her underachievement comes out.

Family Problems

Torie confides that since middle school she has become increasingly aware of and upset by her parents' marital problems. "Probably my mother felt like I was grown up enough to know about stuff like that," she reasons. "She's sick of being married. My father is the domineering one, always bossing everybody around. He tells everyone how to run their life, including us. My mother needs to stick up for herself more." Knowing all this burdens and sometimes overwhelms her.

She worries about whether they will get divorced and what would happen to her. Torie also feels guilty because she believes her parents argue mostly about her. "When I screw up, they really go at it," she says bluntly. For example, her mother is enraged when her father reneges on his threat and allows Torie to go to summer camp despite her poor grades. And whenever Torie sympathizes with her mother and encourages her to be stronger, she feels disloyal to her father. "I can't support either one of them, really, or I'm hurting the other one," she concludes.

Underachieving is Torie's passive way of expressing anger at her parents and punishing them for embroiling her in their marital tension. Also, given her precious little control over her parents' problems, refusing to improve academically lets her grab the reins where she can. Torie may be sacrificing her own success to deflect attention away from her parents' marital strife—or to get help for the family by bringing it out in the open. So although Torie wants to do well in school, she has many unconscious reasons to sabotage her own success.

The Proverbial Straw

Over the next few months, Torie sees me weekly to learn healthier ways to manage the problems in her life. But since her parents are not amenable to family or marital therapy, her home life doesn't change. Just before the end of ninth grade, Torie's boyfriend of nine months breaks up with her, setting into motion a rapid downward spiral. Consumed by grief, she spends most of her time alone in her room. Her parents are sympathetic but unaware of just how devastated she is. Expecting her to rebound, they don't appreciate that she sees this breakup as the last straw.

Brian has been one of Torie's few close friends and her only confidant, the main source of her self-esteem and security. Without her identity as Brian's girlfriend, she feels bereft and lost in school. Going about her daily routine is a painful reminder of his rejection. To avoid not sitting with him in math or biology, Torie begins to skip these classes. To make new connections to her peers, she gravitates to the first group in her school that includes her, the "druggies." Late one Saturday night, Torie sneaks out of her house and takes a taxi to a nearby town where she and her new friends meet up with boys they had met that afternoon at the local mall.

Although Torie's parents are distraught about her rapid decline—as well as her growing hostility and rebelliousness—they refuse to become involved in treatment because they are unable or unwilling to look more deeply into their marriage. But they realize that something has to shift, so they decide to send Torie to a boarding school in a neighboring state.

Unfortunately, Torie goes off before she has the chance to work through her difficulties, much less see the family problems resolved. Moreover, I suspect that while she is away at boarding school she worries about what is happening with her parents at home. Months later, her mother calls to tell me that Torie violated the no-substance policy in her new school. Still trying to deal with her anger and despair, albeit in a self-defeating way, Torie apparently has turned to self-medicating. This is not an uncommon path for teen girls who are unable to more directly address their tumultuous inner lives.

DISTRESSING CIRCUMSTANCES

So many of the distracted girls I see are dealing with difficult living circumstances. As with Torie, many are rather common stresses, such as parental conflicts, residential moves, divorce, or serious illness in the family. But if teens' coping resources are already stretched, these events can become all consuming and destructive. Unbeknownst to their parents and teachers, girls' passions and goals often become entangled in hidden worry, frustration, and resentment. Several situations most commonly distract teens.

Family Changes

It is easy for parents who themselves are immersed in stressful or painful life changes to minimize how much their kids are affected. Ironically, it is usually when parents are most absorbed that daughters need and demand attention, empathy, and support. But as usual, teens give mixed or paradoxical messages, provoking classic push-pull battles with their parents.

Bethany is a prime example. Her parents brought her for an evaluation because she was in danger of failing two sophomore courses. Although they realized she was not able to pay attention, think clearly, or work well, they were unaware of the extent of her underlying unhappiness—or what was causing it.

As an only child of older parents, Bethany spent much time in her room, which had been installed with a computer, a television, and video games. In her free time she no longer would play her cello, but instead would play fantasy games online. Bethany's parents agonized about how to motivate her in school. No matter how much they begged, cajoled, or bribed, she would not heed their suggestions. In a desperate effort to prevent Bethany from "throwing away her potential," her parents offered her money for passing grades and two hundred dollars to take honors math during her junior year.

The evaluation made clear that Bethany's academic decline was emotionally based. Her parents were surprised to learn that this was in fact spurred by their recent decision to adopt a foster child they had taken in the year before. This family change inflamed all the perceived hurts, slights, and wrongs that had accumulated in Bethany's past. In fact, her parents' motivational tactics failed precisely because they reinforced her feelings of being unloved and misunderstood for who she was. Bethany felt truly unwanted.

Although Bethany's parents thought that finally having a sibling, especially a sister, would delight her and make her less lonely, she believed they were replacing her "with a newer, cuter model." She dwelled endlessly on the injustice of her situation. Thinking she could never compete with this adorable toddler for their attention, Bethany's despair and sense of betrayal knew no bounds.

Chatting with strangers on the Internet in the confines of her bedroom proved safer and more satisfying than interacting with real, potentially hurtful people. She could present herself online however she wished and thereby compensate for her growing sense of inferiority. As she described it, "I can be myself, only better. I'm tall and gorgeous, smart and talented. Everybody loves me."

Bethany's crisis unveiled a long history of quiet despair that had been masked by high achievement. Although she had few friends in middle school, she had kept busy with cello lessons, concerts, and competitions. As long as she was getting good grades and winning music awards, her parents and teachers had assumed she was okay.

Apparently, however, she had been a victim of peer ridicule and rejection for many years. The change in her family evoked those same feelings of being rebuffed, stressing her coping ability and provoking a crisis. Overwhelmed and despondent, she withdrew into the sanctity of her room and disinvested in school. Unfortunately, she was so determined to declare her opposition to her parents that Bethany refused to participate in treatment. As she hoped, they then felt powerless to effect any change.

Ongoing Conflict

Chronic conflict is not as obvious a stressor as events such as adoptions, marital separations, siblings leaving home, or deaths, but it can be equally harmful. In Sierra's case, her parents' sudden divorce was not as problematic as their failure to agree on custody and visitation. Bonnie and Greg brought Sierra to see me because she was "a time waster" who would sit at her desk for hours without accomplishing anything. But Sierra was actually doing plenty. Her parents just didn't know how she was brooding and agonizing during those times.

In my office Sierra often asked to draw while we spoke. One day she made a large circle on a piece of paper that she labeled "My Life." Inside she wrote the following words: "depression," "sadness," "distrust," "death," "baby," "orders," "anger," "Meg" (her stepmother), "divorce," "teachers," "parents," "awful," "Dad," and "mean." This drawing spoke volumes, providing a vocabulary for issues that felt overwhelming.

Bonnie and Greg had separated when Sierra was in kindergarten. Both were loving parents who were so devoted to their child that neither was able to surrender a single hour of time with her—or make a single concession to the other. So for six years, while they battled out custody arrangements in a courtroom, Sierra was shuttled back and forth every few days between their homes.

Her parents' legal stalemate—and inability to separate emotionally—harmed Sierra by keeping alive her wish for a reconciliation, arousing her sadness when that never occurred, and inciting her anger when she felt like a pawn in their war. Before one parent session she told me, "Remind them that I am emotional, and when I'm angry, I'm angry, and when I'm depressed, I'm depressed. Sometimes it has to do with them but I can't tell them because I'm scared they'll get angry."

With most distracted girls, intense emotions spill over into their school days, blocking out what is going on around them. Sierra likened this sensation to being trapped inside a cocoon, which kept her from fully connecting with her classmates and paying attention to her work. No wonder she seemed to be spacing out. When Sierra's parents understood the connection to her achievement, they resolved their six-year custody battle over her. After Sierra was released from this parental tug-of-war, she was better able to focus on her own life and use her gifts.

Romantic Breakups

Parents and teachers often view romantic breakups as inevitable rites of passage for girls in high school (and perhaps in middle school), right up there with the first kiss, awkward crush, and school dance. And they are. But that doesn't mean these events are any less distressing, at least for some girls. Even if your daughter only has a boyfriend for a short while, the relationship may be more meaningful to her than you would imagine. There may also be other issues, such as previous losses, that complicate the grieving process. Girls often become weepy, preoccupied, or withdrawn for days or even weeks after a breakup. But if this reaction continues for a month or two without improvement, they may need counseling to get past the loss.

Jessica, a high school senior, was betrayed and devastated when her boyfriend cheated on her and ended their two-year relationship. Like Torie, whose story opened this chapter, she felt terribly isolated when she lost the status of being a couple. By her own admission, Jessica then became "obsessed" with Tim. She reread her diary and mentally replayed their conversations, wondering where she had gone wrong. When she complained, "I feel so stupid!" she was referring to her misplaced trust in Tim, her inability to think clearly since their breakup, and her "pathetic" efforts to get over him.

Having turned her anger onto herself, Jessica felt terribly inadequate in school. This was a huge departure from her early history. "I was always teacher's pet, the smart kid," she admitted. "I did my homework. I never had to work very hard." But her preoccupation stopped her from reading: "I just get SparkNotes now if I have a test or something." To avoid the painful sense of not being on top of her game—as well as sightings of her ex-boyfriend—she began to skip school. "I love to stay in bed all day watching Ricki Lake and Jerry Springer," she told me, with a wry smile.

Even after the initial hurt passed, Jessica still found it hard to concentrate on her work and care about school. She was insightful enough to realize that she had more work to do. The crisis with Tim had brought lingering issues to the surface. "I've always been dependent on boyfriends," she told me. "I've never had enough confidence. I feel like I've never been able to give my opinion to guys, just listened to theirs. Now that I think of it, I've never had my own personality. I've been more a presence than a person." Jessica took a year off before college to work and continue in therapy, giving herself the chance to feel more competent and enthusiastic about her studies.

Traumas

Sometimes parents have no idea whatsoever about the traumas that haunt their daughters. Moira, a junior, said she lost interest in school as a freshman, about a year and a half before I saw her in therapy. "I could be in the top 10 percent of my class, but I don't give it that extra push," she told me. "I used to get good grades, or at least pretty decent grades. I was also the lead in a bunch of middle school plays, and I took ballet for eleven years." Moira no longer pursued any of her hobbies, preferring just to hang out with friends. "I'm not friends with the same kids anymore," she admitted. "My parents don't like my new friends. Not at all."

At the beginning of her freshman year, while visiting a friend where Moira used to live, she spent an evening drinking beer and smoking marijuana with old friends. After going to sleep, she was sexually assaulted by a boy who was also staying over. She never told her parents. But the incident ate away at her, slowly eroding her passions along with her self-regard. She no longer cared about school or performing. "When I'm in a bad mood, it's really bad," she said. "I like to shut out the world." Since then, Moira had begun drinking six to eight beers at least one night per week and smoking pot regularly. "It makes me feel *so* much more relaxed," she explained.

Whatever girls' traumatic experiences, afterward they often feel different—and sometimes damaged. Their recovery absorbs a good deal of their energy and focus. For one, girls usually feel an enormous loss of security, optimism, and innocence. Also, because they believe their troubles irrevocably set them apart from their peers, they feel tremendously isolated. As Moira describes her feelings, "All of a sudden, my friends were, like, these completely different people. They seemed so young, so ridiculously babyish." Girls may be forced to grow up faster, but they feel inferior to peers they consider more "normal."

The Burden of Keeping Secrets

While Moira was intent upon keeping her own secret, many other girls who see mental health professionals feel obligated to keep others' secrets, such as those of their mothers, fathers, and siblings. This is especially true when families teach their kids not to talk with outsiders about what goes on. Also, girls are usually ashamed of the secrets they learn—or how they find out. Girls distracted by such secrets often manifest telltale signs if their parents and teachers know what to look for.

Chris was brought to see me when her grades in middle school suddenly plummeted. Since she seemed tense at the beginning of our session, I asked her to draw a picture before we spoke about why her parents brought her in. Chris's drawing of a girl about her own age was conventional except for having unusually large ears. I found myself musing aloud, "What could this girl be hearing?" That was all the prompting Chris needed; discussing a drawing rather than herself removed her need to censor what was on her mind.

Chris blurted, "She hears her parents whispering in the night. They don't know what she knows." Apparently, Chris's parents were discussing their imminent separation. Not only was she apprehensive about what would happen, but she also felt guilty about eavesdropping. As a result, she was reluctant to reveal to her parents what she knew—or even to confirm that it was true. But keeping this secret upset and drained her. Her declining grades were a tip-off to her distress.

Kayla's situation was even more dramatic. Several years ago, when she was a sophomore, her parents had brought her to me for testing. Slipping grades prompted them to worry that she might have a mild learning disorder. Unlike Chris, Kayla was blatantly hostile, eager to blame others for her situation. "I know I could do better, but I don't care," she said. "It's not like you're going to use this stuff. A lot of it is busy work. Worksheets that are the same over and over. It's an excuse to teach us stuff that they're too lazy to teach us in class." Kayla's over-the-top antagonism suggested that there was more to her story.

Testing ruled out any sort of learning problem that could account for her marked academic decline. Instead, I suspected family dynamics were the cause. Engaged in a battle of wills with her parents, she opted out of studying, stared angrily at her work, and got little accomplished. But she spent much time thinking about what was really going on in her family.

Her parents were caring but intensely private; dealing with their daughter's worrisome grades was easier than addressing their own serious problems. Fortunately, Kayla recognized that she needed to get things off her chest and agreed to come to therapy. It was only then that the secrets of her home life slowly emerged.

Every night after dinner, Kayla ran up to her room and took out the vodka she kept buried under a pile of clothes in her closet. Drinking helped to drown out the noise of her parents' fighting. Getting drunk took the edge off her panic when their arguments turned physical. It also helped her to fall asleep. No wonder Kayla couldn't concentrate on her assignments. By the time they divorced and the family situation stabilized, Kayla's poor work habits and pattern of school failure were more difficult to reverse.

EMOTIONAL DIFFICULTIES

Along with increased stress, teens today suffer from more prevalent and serious mental illnesses that affect their daily functioning and inhibit their success. When girls don't seem motivated or complain that they can't concentrate, many are seen as simply not trying hard enough. But parents and teachers need to be alert to other problems. For example, teens who suffer from full-blown anxiety or mood or attention disorders may look unmotivated, distracted, or apathetic. Unless they are diagnosed and treated, their performance in many areas of their lives could well be compromised.

Depression

Although adolescent moodiness is common, more prolonged sadness, despair, hopelessness, and helplessness may indicate clinical depression. Whereas adult depression is often associated with sleeping and eating disturbances, lethargy, and withdrawal, teens are apt to be restless and irritable, distractible, indecisive, and either hypersocial or isolated. These are not reactions to transient situations, such as transitions or brief periods of feeling insecure, but are more pervasive. Teens may also express morbid or self-destructive thoughts in their creative writing, diaries, or drawings. Many begin to self-medicate with alcohol, marijuana, and other recreational drugs. If parents are in doubt, they should consult clinicians who can decide whether daughters are experiencing true clinical depression.

Depression and its associated self-denigration directly affect girls' abilities. Eva Pomerantz, a psychologist at the University of Illinois at Urbana-Champaign, found that emotionally distressed kids tend to underestimate their own academic and social abilities. Studying self-reported depression and actual grades, she and Karen Randolph found that depressed youngsters in fourth through sixth grades blamed themselves for their failures but attributed their successes to external factors, such as luck. Depression leads girls to underrate their competence, with predictable effects on their success.

What is also important to know is that teenagers who denigrate their abilities often portray a façade of indifference that can be misinterpreted as lack of motivation. Discouragement and help-lessness insidiously undermine girls' achievement. The worse they do in school, the less invested they become. The poorer girls per-form, the more helpless and hopeless they become, until they be-lieve it is impossible to improve.

Anxiety

Anxiety disorders often masquerade as apathy, social-skill deficits, physical complaints like headaches or stomachaches, and refusal to go to school. For this reason, Carla, a sophomore, puzzled all the educational experts, physicians, and holistic specialists whom she and her family had consulted. She suffered from frequent, debili-tating migrainelike headaches; bouts of feeling sweaty, nauseated, and faint; and heart palpitations. She complained that her memory was bad; she couldn't recall simple things. Although medical tests were inconclusive, for two years Carla was treated with intra-venous antibiotics while being homeschooled. Eventually her doc-tors referred her for psychotherapy to explore whether emotional factors were contributing to her illness.

Carla was brilliant. She scored a perfect 1600 on her SATs and earned a four-year scholarship to a state university. But although she aced AP physics, making friends, getting along with peers, and fitting in were hard. Much younger than her siblings, Carla had missed out on typical family interactions and squabbles. In high school she felt out of place when her classmates seemed to talk, laugh, and socialize so effortlessly. Her uneasiness mushroomed into panic attacks, turning her attention from the subject at hand to her palpitating heart and sweaty palms.

This is another example of how emotions affect—and can limit—

thinking. Despite her extraordinary intellect, Carla's emotional state kept her from being fully present, paying attention, and remembering what she heard. That is because when individuals are anxious, their working memory—the ability of the brain to hold on to all information necessary to accomplish a task—is temporarily impaired. Similarly, being stressed out or distracted prevents girls from thinking through problems clearly and remembering what their parents and teachers ask them to do.

Attention Disorders

When difficulties with paying attention are chronic, pervasive, and neurobiologically based, students may have an attention-deficit/hyperactivity disorder (ADHD). Their achievement suffers because they have trouble focusing in class, staying on task, keeping their materials organized, and completing their work on time.

Experts like Thomas Brown of the Yale Center for Attention and Related Disorders consider ADHD a disorder of executive function—that is, the part of the brain that manages cognitive operations. For example, students may have difficulty getting started and understanding directions; focusing, shifting, or sustaining their attention; regulating their effort and their speed of processing information; controlling frustration and other emotions; and monitoring their ongoing behavior.

Girls are not diagnosed with ADHD as often as boys because they are usually not as disruptive, hyperactive, or defiant in class. Parents and teachers less easily recognize quieter signs such as poor concentration, distractibility, and spaciness. This is why girls are more likely to be diagnosed when their symptoms are extreme or when they are difficult to manage—that is, when they fail to follow routines at home or school, seem to ignore requests, or don't respond to corrections.

Alice, a sixth grader I saw some time ago, fit this profile. Her parents described her as extremely immature because she could not get ready for school in the morning without constant reminders. (In fifth grade, she was tardy forty-five times—or the equivalent of nine full weeks of school). Alice rarely started in on her homework when she came home from school. Instead, she procrastinated until the eleventh hour. Just before a book report was due, for example, there would be a sudden flurry of activity, along with predictable frustration, temper outbursts, and tears.

When I observed Alice at her school, she seemed to be in her own world, always a step or two behind her peers. When her teacher directed the class to take out their textbooks and open to a specific page, she looked in her desk and fiddled with her pens. Alice's notebooks were a mess. In the cafeteria she seemed engrossed in her own thoughts. Although she tried to join conversations, she was usually out of step. Alice could not seem to stay organized or in sync with what was going on around her.

Unless ADHD is diagnosed and treated, girls' learning, behavior, and emotional development are affected. Although hyperactivity and fidgetiness often abate during the later adolescent years, symptoms such as disorganization, poor judgment, and difficulty managing emotions may continue. Hyperactivity may be expressed as hypersocial behavior; that is, girls may be excitable, overemotional, and dramatic. They often seek out risks to compensate for poor academic performance and to gain peer acceptance. When I think of girls who fit this description, Jessica comes to mind.

At nineteen, Jessica was at her wit's end. Discussing her long history of school problems, she admitted that she could not always marshal the effort she wanted to. "I thought that when I graduated from high school, things would be different because I knew, I absolutely knew, what I was doing wrong and what I had to do to do better," she told me. "But things are only getting worse." When she got to college, Jessica enjoyed her classes more but found that her difficulties had followed her.

After a dismal freshman year, Jessie was placed on academic probation and came to see me. "My main problems are concentration and following through," she said. "I've taken classes for study skills, and I know them all so well I could practically teach the class. But I don't use them. I make plans, but then I don't follow them." Jessie saw herself as "hyper" and impatient. In class she would usually be first to turn in tests, but would forget to check them over to correct mistakes. Her tendency to overlook the consequences of her actions also resulted in poor judgment outside of school.

Jessie's pattern of skipping classes resulted from her need for immediate gratification and trouble controlling her impulses. She stayed in bed because she was tired and wanted to avoid the anxiety of going to class unprepared. At the end of every semester, however, she faced the crisis of writing late term papers while also trying to cram for her final exams. Each time this happened she would say, incredulously, "I can't believe I did this to myself again."

When girls are suspected of having ADHD, they need a thorough evaluation by a qualified mental health clinician. This diagnosis should be based on detailed academic, social, and behavioral histories; neuropsychological testing; and observations of behavior in school, at home, and in the clinician's office. Individuals with ADHD often look different in various environments. The good news is that once ADHD is identified, there are many treatment strategies that can help students become more attentive, organized, and productive. Teens and their parents benefit when they get as much information as possible from their doctors, books, and the Internet.

It is equally important to avoid overdiagnosing this disorder. One, teens are perfectly capable of being excitable, active, spacey, and rambunctious without ADHD. Two, all teens—including perfectionists, those in transition, square pegs, and insecure girls—daydream or procrastinate in response to stressors. Three, in this era of intense competition for college, an ADHD diagnosis is sometimes used to get students special accommodations, such as extended time on SATs. When incorrectly diagnosed with ADHD, however, girls' real difficulties are never addressed or resolved.

HELPING DISTRACTED GIRLS

► Acknowledge and Address Problems

When girls are distracted, parents and teachers must refrain from making quick judgments about their motivation. Instead, it is important to wonder what preoccupies them. If deeper emotional problems are suspected, professional help should be sought. Parents who are unsure whether treatment is needed should consult with a psychologist or social worker who comes well recommended from a physician, guidance counselor, teacher, or friend. Clinicians can help you decide on the best course of action.

Adults must also take a good, honest look at their own lives. Are there significant conflicts or changes going on in the family? Girls' special antennae let them pick up on these phenomena long before their parents tell them. When you can speak openly, you relieve your daughter of the burden of keeping secrets. Tell her when issues are private and when she is free to talk about them. When your teen knows that you are dealing with problems, they don't fester in her mind.

► Teach Girls to Live in the Moment

Girls who are consumed by their inner thoughts benefit from learning to live more fully in the present. If your daughter is amenable to suggestions, coach her to avoid rehashing the past as well as anxiously anticipating what the future will bring. Instead, she can best resist distractions by focusing on the present.

As Sarah, a middle schooler, describes her situation, "I've learned that if you worry too much about college and the future, you aren't thinking about what's happening right now." Similarly, Mindy, a sophomore, finds that living in the moment offers invigorating freedom. "Last week I was really stressed and couldn't stop thinking about my problems. I decided to go for a walk around the pond with my best friend. I knew I was missing three club meetings," she tells me, "but I wanted to. It was a great feeling, the feeling that the world can wait."

► Keep Problems in Perspective

In the adolescent mind, which can be driven by emotions, troubles are often blown out of proportion. Many girls tell me that the problem that made them think the world was coming to an end one day somehow seemed trivial or even nonexistent the next day. Although it is important to be sensitive to your daughter's desire to be understood and her need to be taken seriously, you might gently encourage her to keep her problems in perspective.

Susan, a sophomore, tells our focus group that she feels empowered by sorting through her problems and deciding what is—and is not—helpful to think about. "If I'm stressing about the fact that I have five tests, or the fight I had with my boyfriend, or why my mom has been sleeping all the time," she says, "instead of flipping out, I calm down and think about what's really important. Which stuff should really be stressful and which stuff I can worry about next week, or maybe never."

► Maximize the Benefits of Downtime

Girls who are grappling with personal and family issues particularly need extra time to rest and recoup. There is no doubt that emotional work is as or more draining than physical labor. When teens are going through hard times, they may need to modify their schedules to ensure they have the chance to relax or to reflect on whatever is bothering them. That way, their preoccupations are less likely to intrude when they are supposed to be concentrating on other tasks or activities.

Along with the relaxation strategies described in the last chapter, another activity that reduces stress and facilitates well-being is writing in journals or diaries. Teen girls have enjoyed this outlet for years, but recent research has identified its emotional benefits. Studying immune functioning in patients with life-threatening illness, psychologist James Pennebaker found that the advantage of keeping a journal comes from actively interpreting one's life rather than merely venting emotions. The healing power of writing comes from organizing, understanding, and learning from one's feelings and experiences.

Thus, girls are more likely to reduce their distress if they use cause-and-effect words such as "because," "realize," "understand," and "meaning." Trying to figure out the positive aspects of stressful situations, making connections between events and feelings, and changing one's perspective are also helpful. Teens who are typically reticent to talk about their problems may benefit most from this kind of personal writing. Educators who teach this approach in school open up extraordinary possibilities for their students.

Imaginative outlets such as art, music, and poetry prove invaluable for teens. As they write, create music, or paint, girls draw upon their inner lives. Their creations promote self-awareness and reflection while helping them to make sense of and manage disturbing thoughts and feelings. Also, creative activities may lead to different viewpoints, fresh possibilities, and new insights. Girls can discover solutions to their problems, inspiring hopefulness and vitality.

Physical activity is always helpful. Although exercise drops off precipitously during girls' teen years, the most resilient students remain active. With Title IX, almost ten times the number of girls played high school sports in 1998 compared to 1971. Girls tell me they walk, do aerobics, kickbox, run, Rollerblade, learn karate, and dance in addition to participating on all sorts of freshman, junior varsity, varsity, and intramural teams.

The benefits of these activities are multifaceted. Girls are better able to tolerate stress, connect with their peers, learn new skills, and manage both collaboration and competition. Sports are known to reduce symptoms of depression and improve self-esteem by releasing endorphins, natural chemicals in the brain that elevate mood. Girls who feel physically fit also report better body images. They learn to value their bodies and respect what their bodies can do for them. Studies show that girls who are active in sports earn higher grades and standardized test scores, are less likely to drop out of high school, and are more likely to attend college.

Although you may not be able to undo your daughter's traumas or resolve all the family's difficulties, there is much you can do to help her manage these stressors as well as possible. Courageously and openly addressing problems, making sure she has a balance of downtime and uses it to her advantage, getting appropriate help, and teaching her better coping strategies go a long way toward making her resilient to distracting personal and family problems.

PART THREE

FOSTERING RESILIENCY

CHAPTER 9

Building Confidence: Knowing Herself

Whatever your concerns are about your daughter or your relationship with her, helping her to be more self-confident will go a long way toward facilitating her success. Girls who feel competent can cope with life's stresses better than those who think they are inept. Self-assurance also allows girls to take the risks necessary to learn and grow. For your daughter to become strong, feel good about who she is, and draw upon her inner resources, she must (1) get to know herself well, (2) think of herself as capable, and (3) believe she can measure up to others' expectations.

You and your daughter's teachers play an important role in this process. She is able to become most self-confident when all of you can stay attuned to her stress level, recognize her uniqueness, and keep your hopes for her appropriate—that is, in line with her true talents. When I think of the mothers and fathers who have worked hard to boost their daughters' self-confidence, Sheryl's parents come to mind.

Without their unwavering support and sensible encouragement, Sheryl most likely would label herself a misfit in her family. A freshman in high school, she is the younger of two children in a long line of highly achieving intellectuals. Her parents are both respected scientists, and her older brother is a Princeton undergraduate. Sheryl, however, is more at home in the sports arena than in the classroom; she lives to play volleyball, soccer, and basketball as well as to snowboard and surf.

Sheryl's parents recognize that she is not—and probably will never be—a scholar. Instead of trying to mold her to the family's blueprint for success, they encourage her to pursue her interests. They educate themselves about her favorite sports, sign her up for teams, and leave work early to watch her games. When Sheryl explores becoming an animal trainer for movies and commercials, they nurture her passion by getting her a puppy and a bird and helping her to find dog-walking jobs in their apartment building.

Despite having an academically gifted sibling and extraordinarily successful parents, Sheryl is self-assured. She tells me, "Sports come easily to me, while other people have strengths in learning and getting good grades. I'm totally different. I might be good at something they're not." Because her parents appreciate her gifts, help her to know herself, and don't expect her to be exactly like them, she feels fine about herself:

> *I know and my parents know that I don't get as good grades. It's pretty unlikely I'll have a straight-A average, but I understand that. My love is sports and animals and having friends, while my brother loves computers and science and math. We have different passions. I don't find happiness in hard work or educational stuff. I get good enough grades and I'm good enough. I've been lucky because my parents haven't tried to make me successful in my brother's way, just in my way.*

Sheryl's parents have given her the empowering message that she has the right to star in her own life. She gets to figure out who she is, what she is passionate about, and where her talents lie. She has the freedom to discover her personal style and to grow from her mistakes. Above all, her mother and father encourage her to get to know herself and to stay closely connected with her inner life. Because they keep their own nervous energy in check, they are able to accept their daughter for who she really is.

STEPPING BACK SO SHE CAN STEP UP

Of course you want your daughter to be as self-confident as possible. But unless you are vigilant, your own history can be an unwelcome intruder. Our past feelings and attitudes, especially during adolescence, shape our present responses to our daughters and their achievement. In fact, whenever girls tell me of parental help that either works beautifully or fails miserably, I suspect the difference is attributable to whether their mothers and fathers are aware of their own biases, needs, and worries. So before you try the suggestions in this chapter to maximize your daughter's self-confidence, take a moment to mentally check in with yourself:

+ Did you experience a defining moment, whether positive or negative, in your school career?
+ Do you wish you had been different back then? If so, what would you change about yourself?
+ Did you make any decisions or mistakes you especially regret? Do you believe they affected your future success?
+ Are you anxious to see your daughter take a specific path that was denied to you?
+ Are you determined to guide her in the way that you wish someone had helped you?
+ When you envision your daughter's success, does a particular college emblem come to mind? Do you obsess about her appearance or activities?

It is especially difficult to feel comfortable with daughters who are different from us or don't match our internal pictures of successful teen girls. Your daughter might prefer the Goth look rather than the feminine, in contrast to what you had imagined. She might be an average or indifferent student rather than the math whiz you had hoped for. She might have one or two close friends instead of the large crowd you had at her age. Or, despite the unmistakable athleticism she got from you, she may shun competitive sports. Still, if your own emotional ducks are in a row, you are best able to:

Encourage rather than pressure her. Does your daughter see your reactions to her achievements as encouraging and validating, or as demoralizing and demeaning? Cory, a senior who swims competitively, offers an example of harmful pressure: "My dad pushes me a lot to be better because he wants me to get a scholarship to college. But maybe he doesn't push me in the best way. He's—well, it's a negative way. It isn't always good. He goes, 'You're never going to make Nationals.' Maybe it makes me try harder sometimes, or maybe I just won't. Sometimes it's, like, 'Okay, that's enough!'"

In contrast, if you can offer guidance without becoming critical or overly invested in the outcome, your daughter will probably perceive that you are more supportive and affirming of her abilities. Robin, a junior, says, "I talked with my dad over the Christmas break about my progress report. We want my grades not to slip, so he asked how I could maintain it. It was an hour and half talk. We had a lot to cover, like colleges I want to look at this spring. It helped me get ready to come back to school."

Stress her goals rather than yours. Do you impose your expectations on your daughter, or allow her to develop meaningful goals for herself? A junior I see in therapy conveyed how quickly parents can slip into the former mode: "When I found out my SAT scores, I told my mom I got a 1380 and she said she thought I'd get a 1500." Any pleasure she got from her score was immediately erased by the

mental calculation of a 120-point gap between her actual performance and her mother's arbitrary standard.

Encourage your daughter to set goals based on what really matters to her. Tessa, one of the freshmen I interviewed, could articulate several well-thought-out reasons for taking honors classes: "I
want to be a lawyer or a judge and you have to do well in school.
Higher classes are more fun too. They teach you interesting
things, and they don't treat you like a little kid. Teachers of higher
classes like their job more because they don't have to deal with the
kids who misbehave so much. Most want to learn." As a result of
this analysis, Tessa is invested in doing well.

When you keep an open mind about what your daughter's path
to success should look like and where she should be at any given
time, she has the freedom to get to know herself. And as you know,
girls can be self-assured only when they know their true strengths
and weaknesses; the route to self-confidence is self-knowledge.
These strategies can encourage your daughter's self-esteem:

Address Her Stress Level

At any given point, your daughter may not be aware of whether she
is coping well enough or whether she is significantly stressed out.
Most girls are pros at hiding their distress not only from you, but
also from themselves. And adolescence is a time of great flux. All it
takes to rock your daughter's social, extracurricular, or academic
worlds is a phone call from her crush, an exciting school assignment, or her coach starting her in a game. On the other hand, feeling excluded, doing poorly on a test despite trying her best, or
getting benched can just as easily deflate her confidence. So getting an accurate read on her stress level requires checking in with
her often.

Although you don't want to overreact to ordinary bumps in the

road, you might wonder if your daughter is feeling stressed out
if she

+ Is especially secretive about her performance
+ Generally rushes around, plays catch-up, and laments hav-
  ing too little free time
+ Never feels like she—or her accomplishments—are enough
+ Is excessively upset by disappointments
+ Complains of feeling overwhelmed
+ Has trouble keeping academics, extracurriculars, and so-
  cializing in balance
+ Dreads school and feels uncomfortable there
+ Twists herself into a knot to please—or has given up all
  hope of trying

Beyond these characteristics, the preceding chapters have clued
you in to the possibility of more specific vulnerabilities. If your
daughter compares herself unfavorably to her friends or siblings,
for example, you might ask if she feels out of place in school or in
the family. If she is frantic to be included in a clique or to find a
best friend, you might talk about whether the desire for acceptance
is adding to her other stresses. If your daughter is never satisfied
with her accomplishments and dwells on doing even better, you
will probably check out whether she feels she has to be perfect. If
she struggles after changing schools, you can point out that she
may be experiencing the normal challenges of transitions. Or if she
seems chronically unhappy, spacey, or sidetracked, you will address
the stresses in her personal or family life that may be distracting
her from success.

If you are still unsure of the pressures your daughter feels or
what she needs from you, ask her. Don't be afraid that broaching
the issue will put ideas in her head or make her more anxious. In
fact, when you ask how she is doing, you are reassuring her that she

is not alone and that many teens feel stressed out. You are also letting her know you are available to talk—as well as giving her the message that you can tolerate this discussion.

Sure she might clam up, especially if she feels as if you're prying or getting on her case. But by keeping your tone light and conveying interest rather than anxiety, your gentle questions are less likely to invoke her wrath. Pick a time when she is usually receptive to talking and say something like "Are you stressed out about anything right now?" or "What can make things easier for you? I know this is a stressful time."

To pave the way for your daughter to come clean about her distress, you might disclose something about your own pressures, as if you're in this together. Or you might use an observation about her friend as a bridge to talking about her—for example, "I heard Liz quit the track team because she's so stressed about college visits. She didn't want the added pressure. How are you handling everything?"

As a next step, you might decide to gather more information. Refer to Chapter 4 for tips on how to contact your daughter's school and ask for feedback on her progress.

Emphasize Her Inner Strengths

When teens think of success, they tend to see a list of accomplishments: stellar report cards, team wins, personal athletic records, invitations to formals, great SAT scores, and acceptances to highly competitive colleges, to name a few. This is true of most stressed-out girls but especially perfectionists and square pegs, both of whom have specific, preconceived ideas about what they *should* achieve.

Far more valuable than helping your daughter to attain these external emblems of success is enabling her to discover her *inner* strengths. What qualities define her as a person? What makes her unique and wonderful? What do you admire most about her? Which traits will serve her well as she makes her way in the world?

For example, tell your daughter if she is fun loving, caring, or a great listener. Let her know you respect her integrity, vitality, or sense of humor. Marta, a high school senior, gets this right: "I don't like tests. They don't show much about you. They don't show how you think. There are other ways to show who you are—like the school's career program, working with kids, and helping out—rather than memorizing." When your daughter believes her self-worth is based more on her inner qualities than on her report cards or SAT scores, you have effectively broadened her tightrope to success.

Research bears this out. At the University of Michigan's Institute for Social Research, psychologist Jennifer Crocker demonstrated that college students who base their self-worth on external sources—including academic performance and appearance—report more stress, academic problems, substance abuse, and symptoms of eating disorders. Although they studied longer, they earned poorer grades and clashed more with their professors. The theory is that people who base their self-esteem only on external sources become anxious and distracted by their academic struggles, which results in poorer performance. Focusing on inner qualities builds a stronger foundation for success.

Emily, a sophomore, realizes that she is far more than her transcript:

> *After a while I realized that grades shouldn't be a measure of self-worth or the only concern of anybody's life. Yes, grades often reflect someone's effort, and yes, they can help with getting into a good college, but other things will start falling through the cracks if grades are number one. My advice to other girls who can't bear to think of anything but a letter grade is: Look*

around. What constantly makes you happy? Your friends?
Family? Crushes? Take a little attention away from your
grades and add a little to these things—a little bit at a time.

Provide Honest and Specific Feedback

Every teen girl needs to know in what ways she shines, in what areas she needs extra effort or help, and the specifics of her personal style. Such self-awareness feeds her confidence and guides her best decision making. To learn about herself, your daughter needs feedback—from you, her teachers, and her peers.

For example, does she tend to be an energetic hard worker? Does she self-initiate, take responsibility, and work independently? Or does she typically slack off, turn passive, and wait for others to help? Your daughter must learn whether she is focused or scattered in a dozen different directions, whether she perseveres or gives up at the first sign of frustration, and whether she is willing to go the extra step or prefers to take the easiest shortcuts.

To help your daughter develop the most accurate picture of herself, give her diplomatic, yet truthful, feedback. The best praise is specific and selective. For example, rather than telling her that she is fantastic or brilliant, point out her improvement in goal tending or writing physics labs. Emphasize the glowing comments on her report cards. Notice when she volunteers to help or pitches in around the house without being asked. Acknowledge her self-control when her sister baits her and she doesn't respond in kind.

But be cautious about exaggerating your daughter's assets. Although girls want their parents to rave about them, they are quick to sniff out false compliments. Toni, a senior, says, "Don't tell me I'm the best at something when we both know I'm not. That just makes me not trust my parents." When I sit down with teens after psychoeducational testing to tell them about their strengths, I often hear, "Yeah, my mom (or dad) told me that too, but I figured they have to say that because they're my parents."

It is especially wise to refrain from well-meaning comments such as "You can do anything you set your mind to." Every girl knows that she has limitations. When you ignore or deny the truth, you lose credibility. Other girls tell me that when they overhear their parents embellishing their accomplishments, they actually feel more inadequate. "What's so bad about coming in third in track?" asks Hillary. "My dad obviously didn't think that was good enough if he had to brag that I came in first."

You can also be honest, though gentle and tactful, about your daughter's shortcomings. Some parents hesitate to do this for fear of damaging girls' self-esteem. However, in my experience the opposite is true. Teen girls are too savvy to be fooled. They already know they are not great at everything and are reassured by the confirmation of their flaws. Feedback helps our daughters to know exactly where they stand and to form the most genuine, realistic pictures of themselves. But avoid offhand comments spoken facetiously, in jest, or out of nervousness. These can act like pinpricks that instantly puncture their pride and self-esteem.

As long as you describe your daughter's weaknesses sensitively, she may feel relieved. For example, if she learns that her reading comprehension needs improvement, she now understands why English has been such a struggle. It is not that she has been lazy or stupid, as she had thought. Or hearing that she tends to interrupt people can shed light on why the girls at her lunch table seem annoyed with her. In fact, instead of making her feel bad about herself, this information prevents her from imagining even worse or more insulting reasons for their rebuff. Feedback also gives her specific ideas about how to set things right.

If your daughter can't trust you to be honest about her weaknesses, she also won't place much stock in your compliments. So if she asks what you think of her social studies paper and you are not impressed, you might say, "The information seems well researched, but the paper needs more careful editing" or "Your thesis is sharp, but the writing isn't smooth yet." Integrating your words with all the other feedback she gets from her teachers and peers, your daughter will form the truest sense of her abilities.

One last comment: Although I have just said that appropriate feedback is vital, sometimes recognition of achievement can backfire. For teens who are excruciatingly self-conscious because they crave peer acceptance, public accolades can be intensely uncomfortable. For those who tend toward perfectionism, too much praise can worsen the unhealthy compulsion to excel. These girls are already worried about what other people think. And once their achievements are publicly recognized, perfectionists feel hard pressed not only to maintain them, but also to surpass them.

For these reasons, schools should rethink the ramifications of posting or publishing honor rolls. And parents might reconsider the wisdom of placing bumper stickers on cars that proclaim daughters as honors students.

Evaluate Her Evaluations Constructively

Since girls spend so much time in school, they judge their success according to their grades. And so do their parents. That is why report cards often provoke such angst, confusion, and misinterpretation. For sure, no topic arouses more emotion in my focus groups. Wendy, a friendly, outgoing freshman, looks crestfallen as she says: "My mom sees the comments and she's, like, 'That's all great, but where are the grades? Let's cut to the chase.'" The following parental approaches to grades help your daughter to appraise and get the most out of her evaluations:

Be Curious Rather Than Judgmental. Responding disapprovingly to your daughter's report cards cuts off valuable self-scrutiny and discussion. Sally, who nervously winds her hair around her finger, describes her father's reaction: "If I get a not-so-good grade, my dad gets upset and lectures you. It makes me feel really guilty. If I get a C, he gets upset. With a B minus, he's not happy." She hesitates, then adds, "His expectations are too high." "I know what you mean," says her friend Zena. "My mom says to me, 'You got an 88? What was the class average? Shouldn't you do extra credit?' Like an 88 is bad?"

When you remain open-minded and curious, your daughter is less defensive and more apt to learn and grow from the feedback offered by her report cards. As Esther, a freshman, puts it, "When I get a bad grade, my parents don't assume I didn't study or fooled around too much. They ask me if I know why it happened."

Monitor Your Expectations. Don't be quick to judge a grade without its context, including the difficulty of a particular class, the idiosyncrasies of every teacher, the current stresses in your daughter's life, and issues such as grade inflation or chance events. Acknowledge those times when your daughter simply can't try harder. Maybe she is getting over a virus and needs extra sleep. Teens in transition are often too focused on a myriad of changes to maintain their usual enthusiasm for a sport or favorite subject. Insecure girls may need to learn about friendship more than biology. Distracted girls usually have to focus on and resolve their problems before they can invest fully in school. Make sure your expectations are flexible and realistic.

Consider the Basis of Grades. It is important for both you and your daughter to consider how her teachers determine her grades.

Does homework count, or are grades based solely upon test and quiz scores? If so, does she typically struggle with certain exam formats more than others?

For example, true/false questions can be confusing to girls who see exceptions and nuances. Fill-in-the-blank items heavily tap memorization and word-retrieval skills, which often tax girls with learning difficulties. Multiple-choice questions are tough for mentally flexible girls who can see shades of gray. Essays require teens to organize larger amounts of information, formulate abstract concepts, and integrate them with supportive facts. Encourage your daughter to ask her teacher or tutor for tips on approaching various test formats most effectively.

Whenever your daughter's grades are partly subjective, they are harder to interpret. For example, if her current English teacher disagrees with what her last teacher taught her about thesis statements, she probably will get lower grades on her papers. Did judgments about her class participation count toward her grade? Was she penalized on a group project grade because of what other students did or didn't do?

A word about effort grades, the judgments about students' motivation and work ethic that often accompany letter and number grades. Although many parents emphasize effort grades, I would suggest caution with this approach. Effort grades are particularly subjective and therefore difficult to gauge. Many times I found my own children's to be more confusing than helpful. For example, how should you interpret a so-so effort mark corresponding to an A or A-plus grade for the subject? Some teachers are philosophically opposed to giving out the maximum effort grade; unless you know this, you might think your daughter isn't trying her best. My advice is not to take effort grades literally; if you have concerns about your daughter's work ethic or habits, ask her teachers directly.

Ask If She Is Satisfied. Parents often wonder, "What should I do if my daughter is doing okay, but I know she is capable of doing better?" This is an excellent question. It all depends on how content *she* is with her performance. Like many parents, you may find yourself in the unenviable position of being disappointed by report cards or athletic performances that your daughter thinks turned out just fine. But now that you are aware of girls' proficiency in hiding their distress, you won't take her blasé posture at face value.

Unfortunately, there is no magic formula for motivating your daughter to want to do better. You can't make her care as much as you do. You can't even make her care. Understanding her underlying pressures and how they affect her performance gives you specific avenues to encourage—but not to guarantee—her success.

For example, girls in transition are so busy focusing on new kids, social opportunities, and challenges and distracted girls are so absorbed by problems that both groups relegate grades to the back burner. Zero in on specific problem areas without chastising your daughter for her apparent apathy. If she is feeling undervalued, for example, she might assume a defiant stance about her grades to cover her fear of disappointing her parents and teachers. Giving her tangible, doable ways to succeed will help to turn things around. Most crucial, your support and affirmation encourage her not to label herself a misfit.

Constance, for example, the daughter of two physicians, is okay with getting mediocre grades at a school for academically gifted students. Although she enjoys the small classes and stimulating discussions with her classmates, she does as little homework and test preparation as possible. Her mother fears that she will have few options for college, but she sees that her daughter is not particularly stressed by her grades. In this case, Constance's needs are being met. Her goal is to go to school with smart, interesting classmates; she is satisfied with not acing her tests.

If your daughter is pleased with her report card, encourage her to recognize her accomplishments and reward herself, if only with a mental "Well done!" If she is not, she has received important information. Then it should be up to her to decide whether to change the material she studies, her approach, or how much time she devotes to her work. Annabelle, an eighth grader, says, "I didn't do very well this quarter in French because I had trouble with the big test. So next time, I'll study more. I think I'll read over my notes from class more carefully because I think that's where I messed up."

Help Her to Set Reasonable Goals. Many girls say they feel like failures. But that is because they are judging themselves against overly vague or broad standards. If your daughter is socially insecure, she may want to be popular. But you may help her to focus first on making one true friend. If your daughter is feeling undervalued in the family because she is hopeless at tennis, her sport may be swimming or skiing. And perfectionists, who aim too high, need their parents to lower the bar for them.

The more *specific* your daughter's goals, the better her chance of tracking her success and feeling accomplished. For example, instead of trying to "do better in school," she should define exactly what she means: finishing her homework every night, writing papers with fewer errors, participating more in class discussions, getting to homeroom on time, or saying hello to people in the halls.

When girls complain of getting "bad" grades and I ask what they were hoping for, I hear of "making honor roll," "getting 100 percent on everything," or "getting straight A's." Whether these goals are realistic depends on your daughter's starting point. It is best to aim for small increments of progress, such as raising a C minus to a C or perhaps a B minus. For this reason, some schools have wisely implemented the BUG roll—an acronym for Bring Up Grades—to recognize students who improve one of their grades without the other grades falling. Struggling students are more apt to feel encouraged if their small achievements are acknowledged with the same respect given to honor students.

Nurture Her Passions

Psychologist Barbara Kerr, author of *Smart Girls: A New Psychology of Girls, Women, and Giftedness*, found that highly successful women fell in love with an idea, "a lasting, often intense, absorbing life-long interest." Dreams direct teens' energy, motivate them to do well in school, inspire their goals, and shape their long-term decisions. When girls are young, they have the luxury of dreaming big dreams and grandiose ideas. As they mature, their mothers and fathers can become anxious about these ambitions, especially if they appear unusual or as mere pipe dreams. Still, your daughter needs you to believe in her and to cheer her on.

As a little girl, Ann Bancroft insisted that she was going to explore the North Pole someday. Her mother supported her by finding adventure books that featured female characters. Playing in her backyard and pretending to be on an Arctic expedition, she honed her practical outdoor skills along with her imagination. Now in her forties, Ann Bancroft is a polar explorer, educator, and motivational speaker. In 2001, she and her colleague became the first women to cross Antarctica on foot. In an interview in the *Daughters* newsletter, she said, "I feel so lucky that I had adults in my life that didn't pooh-pooh me when I told them I was going to the North Pole someday." She is dedicated to furthering girls' explorations and helping them keep their dreams alive.

As your daughter gets older, sprinkle your support with more pragmatic information and guidance. Barbara Schneider and David Stevenson, authors of *The Ambitious Generation*, argue that although today's adolescents are ambitious, they often don't know how to reach their goals. You can encourage your daughter to avoid becoming what they call a *drifting dreamer* by helping her to translate her ambitions into clear, specific, and viable steps.

Does your daughter need to take particular courses in high school? Should she be getting certain experiences now? You might suggest that she read about areas that interest her and arrange for her to shadow individuals whose careers she admires. Perhaps you can match her with a mentor. You can also investigate work opportunities, internships, or volunteer positions that will give her valuable skills and experience.

Parents who believe in their daughters' passions can go all out in making them happen. Erika, a junior, always struggled in school because of a developmental learning disability. Besides socializing with her friends, only one thing excited her: designing clothing and accessories. So her parents got her drawing lessons, enrolled her in a design course at a university forty-five miles away, and taught her to knit. Demonstrating extraordinary focus and perseverance, by age fifteen Erika had developed her own Web site, where she displayed the creations she sold online and in boutiques.

But, you may be thinking, what if my daughter doesn't have any passions? What if she shows no special talents or inclinations, or commits to activities only briefly before quitting? If this is the case, better not to pressure her further. Instead, expose her to as much as possible. You never know when reading a book, hearing a speaker, meeting an intriguing person, or taking a trip will spark brand-new curiosity or inspire a lifelong interest.

Encourage Her to Find Her Study Style

Because of innate variables such as brain wiring and temperament, your daughter brings specific strengths as well as weaknesses to her learning. Although some girls are computer whizzes, geniuses with maps, or have an ear for language, others have to work harder in these areas. In a similar way, your daughter needs to know if she is a born organizer or if she should spend time perusing catalogs from the Container Store. She has to acknowledge if she is a quick study or should plan on doing repetitions and drills before tests. Knowing her learning style is part of knowing herself.

If your daughter is successful, you may be more inclined to trust her instincts. Resilient girls say that their parents don't impose their own learning styles on them. They are happy to give them leeway to figure out for themselves how they perform best, including how, when, and where they should work. If their performance is poor, however, their parents are more likely to question their work habits.

Girls whose styles are alien to their parents often provoke worry. For example, many parents tell me that they can't fathom how any girls, especially distracted ones, concentrate with the cacophonous sounds that emanate from their daughters' bedrooms. Their first impulse is to rush in and unplug the offending CD player or stereo. Yet many girls argue convincingly—especially if they are doing well—that listening to their favorite groups helps. Music is said to act as a natural stimulant, which can keep teens alert, more focused, and less lonely as they do their homework.

Similarly, many parents are aghast at the idea of girls getting together to study for an exam. They can't imagine anything getting accomplished. If your daughter is especially gregarious, desperate for friendship, or dealing with problems that make her feel isolated, she may work more effectively with a study buddy. Bonita, a middle schooler, says, "We divide up the chapters, summarize them, and then we teach them to each other. It really helps us to learn it better and it's way more fun." Being with peers is more stimulating than being alone, and girls are less apt to resent the time that schoolwork takes away from their social lives.

Study Routines. Rather than assuming you already know, explore with your daughter what study routine works best for her. Is she better off tackling her homework right after school, or does she prefer blowing off steam or napping first? Location matters too. Is she most motivated, focused, and productive when she is holed up alone in her bedroom or camped out at the lively kitchen or dining room table? Does your daughter benefit from tackling her hardest subjects first? Although some girls believe, "I like to get my worst subjects over with so then I can relax," others think, "If I do my math first, then I get too frustrated and have to stop."

Time Management. One common dilemma that causes plenty of family drama is how girls organize their time. Many parents I know become wild when their girls procrastinate. They think it is ideal to start early and work methodically, doing a little at a time, until assignments are finished. While this may be your MO, it may be completely foreign to your daughter. Last-minute efforts energize and focus some people. Tammy, a creative and offbeat sophomore, says, "When my fabulous idea arrives, I may devote a whole Saturday or Sunday to a long assignment that's due on Monday."

If your daughter procrastinates because she has trouble getting started, that is another story. In this case you might ask, "Do you want me to go over the assignment with you before you begin?" Many girls appreciate parents who break down tasks into more manageable chunks. Perfectionists, who are notorious procrastinators, welcome clear grading guidelines before they start in. For example, if they know their teachers are looking for certain thesis statements, numbers of pages, and kinds of resources to award an A grade on a paper, they may be less inclined to work as compulsively as they would in search of more elusive grading criteria. If your daughter is adjusting to a new school or different teachers, she may not grasp higher-level assignments and thus will need you to explain directions so she knows what is expected of her.

When it comes to putting her thoughts on paper, which challenges many girls, your daughter has to develop the techniques that work best for her. Although some teens prefer to write the old-fashioned way, with a spiral notebook and favorite pen, others find that computers magically unleash the stream of their ideas. Others find it easier to get started after they write outlines or use visual aids such as Venn diagrams or story maps. Still others need to verbalize their thoughts to someone. Eve, who is in middle school, says, "It helps me to talk out my ideas first with my mom. Saying it out loud helps. And sometimes she writes it down for me."

Tolerate Her Imperfect Behavior

Although most parents want to raise well-behaved and well-mannered kids, the most confident girls are able to show their less than ideal sides. These girls can say what is really on their minds. They can be sullen, annoyed, and even annoying without being stressed out about disappointing people. They feel entitled to debate, argue, and complain. Freedom from pleasing others helps girls to cope more successfully with achievement pressure. Although it is often easier to parent a quiet, submissive teen who doesn't make waves, you might convey to your daughter that having or expressing negative feelings doesn't make her a bad (or unsuccessful) person.

The headmistress of an independent girls' school told me about a confident student whose parents likely agreed with this philosophy: "The editor of our school newspaper is always whining and complaining, but the great thing is, she doesn't care if she pleases me or her mother or her father. She's going to do what she wants to do. She's a great student. She has a great time. She's doing it for herself." Wisely, this woman added, "The ones who whine are safer than the ones who don't. They may make adults irritated, but they're getting it out."

When the girls in my focus groups discuss what they most admire about their mothers, it isn't just their positive, socially acceptable traits they speak about. Kimiko, for example, tells us, "My mom is the strongest woman in the world. It can be such a negative thing. She's very thickheaded and opinionated. But she taught me to be opinionated and strong as well. To stand up for what I believe in. Maybe that causes fights sometimes, but it's okay because I know she'll always support me."

Give your daughter the liberating message that she has to do her work but is not obligated to like it—or to pretend that she does. All girls—and especially perfectionists—need permission to grumble about their teachers, protest the amount of homework they get, and complain about school. By keeping your own nervous energy in check, you avoid becoming alarmed by these remarks. For many girls, expressing imperfect feelings and displaying imperfect behaviors offers an escape valve for tension. Ironically, this enables them to buckle down and focus on their work. Regardless, knowing themselves well requires being in touch with the full spectrum of their emotions.

Give Her the Gift of Time

It is easy to overreact to your daughter's stumbles and setbacks, but try to be open-minded about when her achievements should occur. If you expect success by a certain age or grade level and she doesn't come through, you risk conveying your disappointment rather than waiting it out and allowing her progress to take its natural course. Predictably, the former approach harms her self-confidence.

Maturation plays an enormous role in girls' success. Maybe your daughter's abstract thinking hasn't developed enough yet for her to conquer algorithms. She is not going to shine on the tennis or basketball court by her early teen years if her motor coordination kicks in slowly. But if you believe that learning is a lifelong pursuit—as opposed to a rat race that ends with getting admitted to college or grad school—you are more apt to give your daughter the gift of time.

Stella, a junior, looks like a classic underachiever because she does not fit the mold of a diligent, successful high school student. Though she has a brilliant mathematical mind, she rarely does her assignments, which she perceives as rote, repetitious, and meaningless. When the zeroes she gets for skipping her homework are averaged in with her perfect test scores, she usually gets C's, even in the advanced math and science classes that come easily to her.

Her mother tells me that she has had to make a conscious choice: either to be on Stella's back all the time, checking up on her homework until it's all done, or to let her daughter go through high school on her own terms. Fortunately for Stella—and their mother-daughter relationship—she chose the second option. This mother knows that her daughter won't be able to fully use her intellect or skills until she is passionate about what she does. Stella knows this too. She has been encouraged to know her own mind; she too makes a conscious choice to get mediocre grades with the understanding that she will probably not attend a highly competitive college.

Although you already know that girls mature and develop at different rates, it is hard to be patient with your own daughter, especially if you see her struggling or suffering. But maturation can be wonderful. Try to sit back and watch your daughter evolve. As her brain continues to develop, you might marvel at her new ability to plan, make connections between ideas, use her burgeoning self-discipline, and tolerate frustration. As she figures out who she is, your daughter will gain much-needed confidence. And as you apply the suggestions in this chapter, she will use that self-knowledge and assurance to discover her passions and ideals.

When all this comes together, she is most likely to succeed in whatever she does. Until then, I suggest following psychologist Harriet Lerner's no-nonsense, straightforward advice to parents; in *The Mother Dance*, she writes, "Children move forward according to their own timetables and not in a predictable fashion. . . . You cannot predict your children's future. No matter how terrible (or well) they appear to be doing now, you don't have a clue as to how they will turn out over the long haul."

What you can be sure of is this: Giving your daughter permission to know herself well and to remain authentic allows her to enjoy learning and achieving. She is more likely to experience the thrill of an Aha! moment when she finds a creative solution to a problem. She is better able to relish the sweet satisfaction that comes from accomplishing something important. And beyond her degree of success, staying in touch with herself has tremendous psychological benefits. Your daughter's awareness of her feelings and ability to express them appropriately is an antidote to many of the mental health problems that specifically afflict young women today.

CHAPTER 10

Creating Connections: Empowering Relationships

No matter how intelligent teens are, those who are able to create healthy connections—with friends, classmates, teachers, coaches, tutors, and mentors—are better able to cope with harmful pressures to succeed. Along with strong self-confidence, caring relationships are another powerful antidote to stress. That is why socially immature girls and those with less developed interpersonal skills are at greater risk for feeling not only isolated, but also more stressed out and less accomplished during adolescence.

To enhance children's resiliency to stress, the American Psychological Association recently initiated a public-education campaign. Along with developing teacher and parent materials, they designed a magazine insert for fourth, fifth, and sixth graders that addresses self-confidence, optimism, and active planning and goal setting. Above all, the program emphasizes the need for motivating beliefs, which were discussed in the last chapter on self-confidence, and stress-reducing relationships, which this chapter focuses on.

Many resourceful teens develop strong people skills. Whether or not they are brilliant or book smart, they have social smarts. Insight and empathy help girls to understand themselves and others. Their abilities to read nonverbal cues, analyze unspoken motivations, and monitor their own feelings guide their behavior. Communicating effectively, they can discuss problems and resolve conflicts. Thus the most resilient girls are able to maintain the sorts of relationships with peers and adults that empower them, direct their efforts, and support their accomplishments.

Good interpersonal skills also have been linked with academic achievement and intelligence. In one study, for example, psychologist Adrian Raine and colleagues discovered that children who by age three had explored their surroundings and initiated social interaction (defined as speaking to strangers) not only had better grades and reading skills at age eleven, but also enjoyed an average of twelve more IQ points than those who as toddlers had sought out less social stimulation.

What this research suggests is that if you want your daughter to be successful, helping her to build good social skills and to maintain healthy relationships is more valuable than giving her extra French lessons, sending her to intensive soccer camps, or hiring expensive SAT tutors.

Of course, not all resilient teens are outgoing. Some are shy, but they bond with at least one other peer—boy or girl—who becomes a treasured best friend. Also, it is not that less socially connected teens don't excel academically; there are always middle school and high school students who remain on the fringe of their peer groups, yet get fine grades and go on to lead productive, successful lives.

Psychologist Barbara A. Kerr, who studied eminent women, found that many felt socially unsuccessful as adolescents. For example, having poor social skills upset Eleanor Roosevelt, Georgia O'Keeffe rebuffed her peers before they could reject her, and Margaret Mead felt ignored and unpopular. As girls, they had exhibited a degree of social awkwardness that, if observed today, might cause their parents to run for professional help. Yet they all went on to become extraordinary women.

But for girls with disappointing social relations, the middle or high school experience is a whole different animal. As expressed by the girls whose stories fill this book, they often suffer silently throughout years that feel absolutely tortuous. Although all teens go through rough patches, square pegs, by definition, see themselves as painfully different from their peers. Girls in transition are often frantic to form new friendships or maintain old ties. Feeling unaccepted chronically preoccupies insecure girls. And perfectionists alienate their peers if they can't tolerate other people's flaws any better than their own.

Whether your daughter is showing signs of one or more of these at-risk patterns or is more generally stressed out, stronger relationships can temper her distress. This chapter describes the school climate most conducive to greater connectedness, as well as what administrators, teachers, and parents can do to bolster girls' social skills and encourage them to develop healthier relationships.

A POSITIVE SCHOOL ENVIRONMENT

When psychologist and author Daniel Goleman discusses the sort of school culture that encourages students to develop people skills or *emotional literacy*, he suggests building "a place where students feel respected, cared about, and bonded to classmates and teachers." Essentially, he is describing a supportive community.

The teenage girls I speak with wholeheartedly agree. When it comes to their feelings about school, there seems to be no middle ground: Either they feel safe and cared for, or they are unhappy. Danielle, a *Girls' Life* reader who is a freshman, vividly describes what it feels like for girls in less than ideal school settings:

> *I have had to adjust to two new teachers so far this year, which I think adds to the stress. My homeroom teacher was moved across town because he was accused of sexual harassment. My*

German teacher retired unexpectedly, and now we have this
teacher who can't speak English and no one is learning any-
thing. Today, two students were kicked out for "being bad,"
and neither of those two students deserved to be moved. Our
principal is recording our class now. It is rather depressing to
start your school day off with total and utter chaos. So, for me,
learning isn't fun anymore, which is unfortunate.

Not surprisingly, when I ask teens about the one thing they would change to make their school experiences better, girls (but not boys) want to strengthen their ties with the people they see daily and improve the social climates of their schools. For example, girls in middle school and high school say they would like

+ "Nicer friends and teachers."
+ "More empathic friends."
+ "Friendlier people."
+ "Fewer cliques."
+ "Closer relationships with faculty and staff."
+ "More caring and helpful teachers."

These findings dovetail with data from the National Longitudinal Study of Adolescent Health, the most comprehensive study ever conducted of American adolescents and their parents. Psychologists at the University of Minnesota found that schools with positive climates—characterized by factors such as well-managed classrooms and moderate disciplinary policies—may reduce teens' emotional distress along with their risk of substance use, deviant behavior, violence, and pregnancy.

The key factor is students' sense of attachment to their schools. Although most students in most schools reported feeling connected, a staggering one third of teens feel disenfranchised. As you wonder whether your daughter's school environment facilitates connectedness, consider the following findings:

School Characteristics

It may surprise you that school type—whether your daughter attends a public, private, or parochial school—has been found to have no effect on the connectedness of students. Neither does class size. Even the level of teachers' educational experience has no impact. But the size of the school matters. When schools are smaller (ideally, fewer than six hundred students), kids feel more connected because there is more personal contact among students, faculty, and administration. Theoretically, the better girls and their teachers get to know one another and feel comfortable with one another, the more likely they are to develop personal relationships.

Classroom Management

How classrooms are managed is also vital. Students feel more connected when they are treated as valued members of the school community. Teachers make this happen when they consistently acknowledge every student—not just the highly achieving ones or personal favorites. Teens also feel respected when they are allowed to manage themselves rather than being micromanaged. For example, they appreciate having input on curricula, classroom rules, and grading criteria. They also feel more connected to schools with moderate—rather than strict, harsh, or zero-tolerance—disciplinary policies.

Social Inclusion

The University of Minnesota study also found that connectedness is associated with social inclusion. Students who feel most integrated with their schools have friends in class, across race and gender, and in overlapping cliques. Connected teens are also involved in extracurricular activities. These factors go hand in hand. The safer and more accepted teen girls feel in school, the more apt they are to join in; and the more they participate in school-related activities, the more connected they feel to their peers, teachers, and administrators.

A TOLERANT SCHOOL CULTURE

In my experience, what enables this kind of involvement is a tolerant school culture in which girls feel less pressure to fit in and conform. The road to social success is not a tightrope, but a wider, less precarious path. In relatively open-minded middle schools and high schools, for example, girls believe that social inclusion and popularity are determined by more than superficial or elusive qualities. They think it is okay, perhaps even cool, to be smart. Roles in the school play, math prizes, and creative writing publications are valued along with softball trophies. Social acceptance isn't determined by a certain brand of jeans, a boyfriend from the popular crowd, or being seen at a particular party.

Addie describes her high school as inclusive: "There's not a vicious popularity thing going on here. This group of guys and girls has been friends since elementary school. It's not about money or clothes. You don't have to have blond hair or blue eyes. It's how long you've known them and if you mesh well together."

There is a similarly nonjudgmental attitude about body type that is liberating to these teenage girls. "Skinny isn't a requirement," announces Suzanne, a senior in one of my focus groups. "Just be toned, not enormous, and wear something flattering for *you*." She adds, "A lot of people are trying to see what's healthy and better for people." This outlook encourages girls to reach out and make friends.

Ella, on the other hand, portrays a harsh high school climate that discourages girls from feeling socially included: "The type of girls who some call nerds, the ones who always eat alone and in others' point of view hit their heads on lockers and snort, my guess is the pressure for them is fitting in. Every popular girl in school makes fun of them in different ways, like for their clothes."

WHAT ADMINISTRATORS CAN DO

To foster students' connectedness with school, the same University of Minnesota researchers offered numerous recommendations for administrators, including:

+ Turning mistakes into learning opportunities rather than punishment
+ Honoring accomplishments and competencies of all kinds, including helpfulness, good citizenship, improved performance, volunteerism, participation in decision making, and cessation of negative behaviors
+ Reinforcing expectations for positive behavior and academic success
+ Inviting all students, family, and community members to take active roles in the daily operation of school
+ Creating and displaying a common vision of success

In addition, I believe it is important for school administrators to heed parents' and teachers' concerns about the social well-being of students. It is essential that they listen carefully to students who report incidents of being disrespected or harassed. They might, among other approaches, invite speakers to discuss social issues affecting teens and establish age-appropriate programs to reach out to alienated or socially immature students, such as social skill building or lunch-bunch groups.

WHAT PARENTS CAN DO

For parents who want to encourage their daughters' connections in school, the study suggested the following strategies:

- ✦ Be a model of respect, cooperation, and positive behavior in all interactions with the school.
- ✦ Show interest.
- ✦ Participate in school events.
- ✦ Maintain regular contact with teachers.
- ✦ Be present when things go wrong.
- ✦ Volunteer at school and support school leaders.

This all sounds good in theory. But in the real world, the guidelines for if, when, and how to get involved appropriately in your daughter's educational world are probably getting blurrier and more confusing by the day. For one, you may be finding that now that she is past the elementary years, her school may not ask for your involvement or be as receptive to your requests. You probably have less contact with your daughter's various teachers. It also may be challenging to fully support your daughter's school if she is struggling academically or socially, if she and a teacher are clashing, or if you have philosophical differences with the administration.

Your daughter, too, may be giving you different—more likely, mixed—signals about how much she wants you involved in her school. The girl who used to enthuse about your being Class Mother, making costumes for the play, or demonstrating the dreidel game at the annual holiday party may become apoplectic whenever you show up on school property. This attitude is a normal reflection of your adolescent daughter's need for autonomy, but doesn't have to exclude you from the information loop.

Perhaps a more delicate and tactful approach is needed. Rather than being a weekly volunteer in the classroom, for example, you may have to find alternate (that is, behind-the-scenes) ways to stay involved and in the know, such as working at the book fair, editing the school newsletter, attending parent-teacher organization meetings, volunteering backstage, or serving on the school board.

By keeping you in touch with teachers and other parents, these activities will add to your reservoir of information. To avoid upsetting your daughter, ask her in advance how she would feel if you sold tickets to an upcoming dance or acted as a chaperone. You might reassure her—"Don't worry, I won't look all over for you or hang out with your friends!"—and agree beforehand on the nature of any contact you will have with her during such events.

It is still hard for parents to assess how a daughter's school culture influences her sense of self and ability to relate to others. It is a challenge to sift through a teen's complaints, problems, and hurt feelings to ferret out signs of potentially serious or pervasive discomfort. But the bottom line is, does your daughter believe she is in a caring place where teachers and administrators listen to students, take their concerns seriously, and are emotionally available to them?

Pay close attention to what she reports during the school day, as well as what details she omits. Be especially alert to stories of striking inequality, incidents that make her feel stupid or insignificant, or her capitulation to policies or values to which she is usually opposed. One surefire sign of an uncomfortable, if not harmful, situation is your daughter suddenly turning negative about school.

This was brought home to me many years ago when my own

daughter was in fifth grade. Initially, I didn't take too seriously her complaints about her first male teacher. But eventually my ears perked up. Some of his remarks did seem odd and even inappropriate. He did seem blatantly biased toward boys. Then my daughter began to report that her male gym teacher made the boys into game captains because "they know the rules better" and penalized girls—but not boys—who forgot their sneakers.

Finally, I realized something had to be done. With my coaching, my daughter decided to speak to her principal, a gentle man who nodded sympathetically but did nothing. Then she and a group of girls began to commiserate with each other. This prompted them to band together, get up their nerve, and knock on the door of the guidance counselor, a passionate and opinionated woman who was outraged by what they told her. Whether or not real changes occurred at school, what made all the difference to these girls was knowing that their parents and at least one authority figure at their school would listen to them, validate their concerns, and support them.

There are times when it is necessary for parents to intervene. If your daughter's attempts to rectify problems with school personnel are unsatisfying—or, worse, if she feels dismissed or diminished— you may have to step in. Mia, a junior at one of the large public high schools in which I conducted focus groups, reported an intolerable situation that made her second-guess herself and feel unsafe in school:

> One of the security guards was following me, so I went to my guidance counselor and they brought in this social worker and more people and they didn't believe me. They did an investigation, but they basically asked people about my personality, like do I exaggerate? So I don't even tell them anymore. I just ignore it. Besides, why should he follow me when there are so many people who are more beautiful?

THE IMPORTANCE OF TEACHERS— AND WHAT THEY CAN DO

Among other strategies, the University of Minnesota study recommends that teachers interested in fostering students' connectedness to schools:

+ Be attentive to their students;
+ Give students more say in what they will learn;
+ Involve them in planning, problem solving, classroom chores, grading, and other responsibilities;
+ Promote cooperation over competition.

Based on my research and clinical experience, I believe the most important thing educators can do is to *develop strong relationships with each of their pupils.* From listening to teen girls, I find it clear that their teachers, mentors, and coaches influence and, in some cases, determine their success. Does your daughter find her teachers supportive and helpful? If she feels good about these connections, she believes her teachers value her and expect her to succeed. With less stress and greater self-confidence, she is more likely to make an effort in school.

Girls are clear about the importance of relationships with teachers. Katie, a middle school student, says she is most successful when she has "teachers who talk to you and care about that you do good in school." Amelia, who is the same age, explains: "If you like your teacher, you want to do better in their class. And if you talk to your teachers more, you have a better chance of doing better because they'll help you more."

Even during high school, your daughter's achievement still depends upon how well she connects with her teachers, her feelings about them, and her perceptions of how they feel about her. Sometimes an especially mature, self-directed teen aces a class in spite of—or perhaps because of—a teacher she dislikes. But that is rare. More often, girls go through entire school years stoking the fires of their disgruntlement with ever-mounting proof of their teachers' shortcomings. Maintaining this posture uses up energy that could be channeled more valuably.

Skilled teachers recognize this self-defeating pattern and try to help girls turn things around. If your daughter's teacher doesn't reach out, or if she is unable to respond to such overtures, you may have to get involved (see "Resolve Conflicts Effectively," page 251). But somehow, encourage her to develop and maintain strong relationships. For girls to thrive and feel most successful in the classroom, their needs may have to be approached differently from those of boys. Specifically, they need their teachers to do the following:

Build Trust

Teen girls must feel safe with their teachers, mentors, and coaches. They have to trust that adults will respect them, listen to them, and, above all, protect them from humiliation. For this reason, it is critical to create a secure environment—whether in the classroom, art studio, stage, or on the ball field—in which no form of discrimination, teasing, or disrespect is tolerated. Belinda, a freshman, describes the benefits:

> When I like my teacher and think they like me, I'm more comfortable in class and can talk to them. If I think a teacher hates me, I won't ask questions. Some people in my class call

other people stupid. It's not right. I'm always scared that will happen and I'll be embarrassed. But if the teacher likes me, I don't think I'm going to get embarrassed.

It is no exaggeration that a casual comment or insensitive correction from an adult can feel like the final word on a girl's self-worth. Teens report feeling most embarrassed in school when they are teased, don't know an answer, feel helpless, or have a teacher publicize their grade. Although girls usually keep their humiliation hidden, it continues to threaten their ability to trust for some time.

Thus, it is key for teachers to address the rumbling of negative commentary in the classroom that immediately silences some girls. It is also crucial to ensure students' privacy when distributing and discussing grades and test scores. Being singled out for either exceptional or poor performances can equally embarrass girls. Similarly, coaches must be mindful of teasing and so-called playful put-downs in the athletic arena that undermine girls' self-confidence and security.

Mary Monroe Kolek, an assistant superintendent of a Connecticut public school system, advises teachers not to use sarcastic humor or disrespect other teachers, even subtly. When kids hear their teachers making such negative comments, they believe they may be next and conclude that the school environment is unsafe. A secure school culture is necessary for girls to interact freely, feel included, and thrive.

Monitor Social Dynamics

When teachers are aware of happenings in their students' social lives, they are best prepared to deal with or circumvent problems. It is important to consider possible reasons for undesirable behaviors like girls suddenly switching seats, whispering feverishly, becoming emotional, or refusing to work with certain classmates. These behaviors may not be acts of purposeful disobedience, but rather indications of troubling social dynamics affecting girls' performance. Teens who act out or make jokes may be looking for peer attention or approval. Those who arrive late to class may be avoiding harassment in the hallways. Girls who want to leave class early or see the nurse are often upset about social crises.

Be Available

Asking for help is particularly difficult for teens who want to be seen as competent and independent. Among girls' worst school experiences are also "being overwhelmed in class and receiving no help from a teacher who felt that my struggle would only build character" or "my teacher telling me just to try harder."

Girls appreciate and respond to teachers who are receptive to their questions and seem willing to go the extra mile. This availability makes teens see their teachers as on their side. When teachers graciously offer to help, girls feel less stupid, needy, or burdensome. Sally, a sophomore who struggles in math, nonetheless says her math teacher is her favorite:

> *Some teachers, if you have a question they won't want to talk about it. They'll say, "Let's talk about it after class." But then you have to make arrangements to stay after school and it's a nuisance. Like, you may have something or they may have a meeting. That's why I love my math teacher. If you have a question on something, he'll go back. If five people don't understand, he'll go over it five times until everyone understands it. All you have to say is, "I'm confused."*

When asked in an interview what they would change to make their school experiences better, many girls spoke of getting more help:

- ✦ "I could talk to any of my teachers if I don't understand the material."
- ✦ "Change one thing? Have help every week studying."
- ✦ "Help me, encourage me, tell me what I'm doing right or wrong."
- ✦ "Teachers to open themselves to more help."
- ✦ "Get my questions answered."
- ✦ "Ask for extra help from teachers."
- ✦ "For teachers not to intimidate me, so I wouldn't be scared to go in and see them."
- ✦ "Teachers—don't get mad when students ask questions."

Give Individualized Support

When girls form personal connections with their teachers and coaches, these adults get to know them as individuals and can guide them to use strategies that are most appropriate for them. Jan says, "I learned so much from my Spanish teacher in just the first month. She gave you a sheet of paper and a quiz. She let you grade it yourself. Then she would let you retake it—the exact same quiz. It helped me so much. I learned so much."

Similarly, Isabella, who is in middle school, has learned from past experience that she needs individual support to learn certain subjects. "Some teachers help me to study better to get better grades," she tells me. "I meet them during study hall and they review everything with me. My math teacher makes it easier because he's willing to help you. I can ask questions and stuff." She speaks for many girls when she clarifies, "I *can* ask in class, but I *don't*."

Teachers, coaches, and mentors help girls enormously in their efforts to succeed by providing feedback about their performance. How that feedback is given matters greatly. Girls thrive when they find out what they did *right* as well as what they did wrong and, specifically, what they can do to improve in the future.

What also helps teens, especially when they hit a wall, is when adults take responsibility for their part in a situation. Teachers who acknowledge their contribution encourage students to do the same. Mimi says, "I got a D on my science test, so I went back and talked to my teacher. He let a bunch of us come back before school or after school to take a retake. I got a B. A lot of the material was stuff he didn't give us. That's why my teacher let us." Mimi's respect and gratitude for her teacher led to her success.

Recognize and Accept Girls' Limitations

It is equally important to recognize that teen girls—like everyone else—have limitations. And that is okay. If students have more than two tests or projects due in the same day, for example, they may feel hopeless about succeeding. That is why it is important for adults to be aware of the potentially overwhelming pressures of crunch times: during midterms, finals, and before the ends of marking periods. Not every girl can excel under these stressful conditions.

For your daughter to truly connect with her teachers, they have to know who she really is—her limitations along with her strengths. Although many parents want to present their kids in the best possible light, schools can best help if they are aware of students' weaknesses and challenges, their learning styles, and which strategies worked in the past. So although your daughter should have the chance to make a new start every year, if necessary, you should make her teachers aware of her typical patterns and idiosyncrasies.

MAXIMIZE YOUR DAUGHTER'S SOCIAL SKILLS

Your daughter's school's climate and the availability of her teachers affect whether she builds strong social connections. If she is feeling disconnected, you may question whether she is in the right place (more on this in the next chapter). But her social skills count too. Developing strong bonds with teachers and classmates is a two-way street. No matter where she goes to school, help her with the following:

Respect Authority Figures

When girls come to school with positive attitudes, their teachers find them enthusiastic learners, and their coaches see them as cooperative team players. Girls can disagree with their teachers and administrators, but they have to do so in ways that convey respect and therefore preserve these relationships. Teens who feel undervalued sometimes show up with chips on their shoulders that evoke the very responses from teachers that they fear most. Those who are distracted by chronic family discord often act out their anger and resentment on other adults.

Does your daughter view her teachers as valuable resources or as potential oppressors? Is she predisposed to listen to adults and do what they ask? Can she respond to constructive criticism without feeling personally attacked?

If your daughter is unaware that her attitude is disrespectful, dismissive, or off-putting, she needs corrective feedback. Don't be afraid to share your insights along with what her teachers observe. Try "I heard something that might be helpful to you." Then repeat the comments succinctly, without editorializing or passing judgment. Even if your daughter denies what you say or your input seems to fall on deaf ears, she is hearing it.

Ask Appropriately for Help

The most resilient girls know how to reach out to adults who take an interest in them and encourage their talents. Socially skilled girls are better able to elicit support and cooperation from others. They know whether teachers prefer to be e-mailed or consulted after school. Whether they want to improve their next biology lab or review the steps in a geometry proof, they ask in ways that ensure they get that help. And they keep asking questions until they get answers.

Can your daughter ask for what she needs? Does she behave in ways that make people feel good about helping her? If your daughter is too shy, self-conscious, or anxious to approach adults, she is not alone. Many teen girls need practical strategies. What should she say? What shouldn't she say? Try role-playing to make her more comfortable. Also, share pertinent stories from your own life that illustrate how you prevailed when it was difficult for you to ask for help.

Maintain Healthy Friendships

Socially adept girls are selective about which classmates they want to befriend, which to keep as school acquaintances only, and which to distance themselves from. Some teens deliberately seek friends who are good influences—that is, they may enjoy socializing, but they also care about their school performance. Fiona, a middle schooler, says, "My parents expect me to do well and I do, mostly. To help, I hang out with the smarter kids that feel the same way about school that I do, so I don't have to worry about them thinking that I'm a drag if I have to do my homework."

Parents rarely find fault with this approach. More typically, however, mothers and fathers become anxious when their daughters befriend kids who are not achievers. It is usually unhelpful to point out to your daughter the disadvantages of such friendships; to demonstrate their autonomy, in fact, girls sometimes cling to unhealthy friendships only because their parents condemn them.

It should be reassuring to know your daughter is unlikely to catch the indifference of her less academically inclined friends. The more you have encouraged her to know herself, to stay in touch with her true desires, and to feel good about her accomplishments, the more immune she will be to negative influences. Clara says:

> It may sound selfish, but as you grow you focus on yourself more. You're aware of everybody else, but you try to increase your own strengths and what you need to do to improve. What everyone else does starts to be less important. You have to be who you are and be happy with what you do. Freshman year I was so focused on whatever everyone else thought. It's weird to look back. I feel a lot different.

Also, if you see your daughter disentangling herself from old friendships, don't panic. This is most likely a healthy move. In fact, recent research counteracts the old notion that teenagers who switch social groups are in trouble. In one longitudinal study, three quarters of the peers whom high school seniors named as their closest friends were not even mentioned during these students' sophomore year.

Teenagers who made changes in their friendship circles cited adaptive reasons: they changed interests or activities, encountered conflicts, changed classes (and, therefore, classmates), wanted more fluid groups, and tried to avoid contact with drugs and alcohol. In my experience, teen girls most often change social groups when they are uncomfortable with their friends' values or activities.

If your daughter feels disconnected, encourage her to participate in after-school activities. Getting involved in chorus, stage crew, or community service lets her mingle with students whose shared interest can become the basis for friendships. If she is still reluctant, meeting the teachers in charge of the clubs could ease the way. If there is no late bus in the afternoon, offer to pick her up after her activity or arrange for a car pool so that she is not burdened with finding transportation.

Avoid Alienating People

Socially skilled girls can maintain relationships because they can get their needs met while remaining respectful of others. For example, they offer their opinions and even debate without alienating their peers or adults. They steer clear of making arguments personal, putting people down, or being condescending. What guides them is their ability to read others' emotional reactions and monitor their own behavior.

Girls who are eager to fit in at new schools or those who struggle with more chronic insecurity sometimes try too hard and strike the wrong note. They may seek attention and approval through silliness or put-downs or meanness. Does your daughter stick up for herself without becoming nasty or hostile? Can she avoid blurting out insensitive or offensive comments? Does she listen attentively to others without interrupting or becoming argumentative? If she hears her voice getting too strident or sarcastic, does she tone it down? It is important that she gauge the effect she has on others.

Work Well in Groups

For many girls, the chance to work on assignments or projects in groups is a reprieve from being sentenced to study in solitary confinement. But collaborating with classmates requires more advanced social skills. Girls must be able to contribute to discussions without monopolizing airtime. They have to balance being creative with staying on track. Does your daughter initiate partnerships? Can she work cooperatively? Is she a team player? Or does she take over, do all the work, and then feel resentful? Can she take stock of her partners' strengths and use them toward the common goal?

The most socially skilled girls (and perhaps future managers) use diplomacy and fairness to divide tasks effectively, foster group decision making, reach a consensus, and forge cohesion. If your daughter lacks these skills, provide her examples of good leadership and cooperation from your school or work experience. Share with her what you have learned from biographies of successful leaders—or read one together. Consider signing her up for a summer program that develops group cohesion and leadership skills, such as those offered by volunteer groups or Outward Bound.

Manage Competition

In the best of worlds, girls benefit from healthy competition. They enjoy the camaraderie of working with friends and rally around each other to boost everyone's performance. Jade, a sophomore, describes, "Last year in bio, there was a big competition with our grades. It made us do so well. We'd do everything together, then we'd break up and have this huge competition. If someone did bad, we'd laugh about it. It boosted our motivation. It was a friendly competition."

With the high level of nervous energy circulating today, however, many girls find it hard to manage the competitive feelings that academics and sports engender. Since they believe their future success is hinging on every single grade, win, or award, seeing others' accomplishments can inflame their insecurity and threaten their relationships. For perfectionists, the need to be the very best makes everyone a potential competitor.

Socially skilled girls keep their relationships on track by monitoring the competition between their friends and themselves. They prevent themselves from being cutthroat. When they surpass a friend, they pay close attention to her facial expressions, tone of voice, and body language to sense whether she is feeling threatened or insecure. As always, though, socially skilled girls walk a fine line. "If my friend is in trouble," a high school sophomore told me, "I'll help her out. She can rely on me. But you also don't want to rub it in their face if you do better."

The most resilient girls are also aware of how they react to others' successes. They know that when they get back grades, they look around for clues as to how they performed compared to their friends. According to one middle schooler, "If my best friend is smiling, I think she's happy and she must've done better than me. Maybe she's just smarter." Another told me, "Every time a test is handed back, people ask me what my grade is. I'll admit I do that too. And the annoying thing is that maybe I'll get a B and I'm happy with it, but then someone gets a B plus and complains, you know?"

Ideally, girls learn to accept that they will not always be first or best. They stop looking over their shoulders. Some even begin to take joy in their friends' accomplishments and talents. Sasha, a junior, tells me:

> *As a freshman, I really wanted to do well. I was seriously hurt when other people didn't do anything and got better grades than me. Some people go out every day after school with their friends and still make honor roll. Now that I've gone through high school for a while, I know myself as a student better and I've gotten used to the way things are. I know my friends' strengths and weaknesses, and I just take it at that. I know Jen always gets an A. It's okay.*

Resolve Conflicts Effectively

Addressing issues skillfully—clearly, tactfully, and directly—socially skilled girls are often able to avoid many of the misunderstandings that plague less communicative teens. If your daughter is able to express her feelings appropriately—including negative emotions such as disappointment, anger, and frustration—she is two steps ahead of the game. The ability to avert social crises also protects her from the emotional upheavals that typically accompany them. With fewer distractions and less drain on their mental energy, as described in Chapter 6, girls who are secure in their relationships are better able to focus on and invest in whatever they are doing.

Of course, no relationship—either with peers or adults—is free from conflict. When clashes do occur, the more adeptly your daughter can address and resolve them, the better she can keep her relationships on an even keel. What can you do to help? Perhaps when she was younger you called her friend's mother and tried to work things out. Now that she is a teenager, however, that level of involvement is inappropriate—unless she is involved in bullying or harassment, in which case you will report this to the authorities at her school.

What you can do is listen attentively. Recap her viewpoint and clarify her feelings. If your teen wishes, help her brainstorm solutions. But think twice before offering unsolicited advice. Also, be cautious about pointing out how her friends are probably feeling, because she might interpret that as evidence of your taking their sides. When you encourage your daughter to take age-appropriate responsibility for working out the snags in her friendships, you are conveying your faith in her social skills.

Repeated conflicts with her teachers will eventually erode her alliances with them. Take the position that blaming teachers won't help. Instead, encourage her to work things out. Let her use you as a sounding board for thinking up possible solutions. Perhaps if she changes her approach in some way, her teacher will too.

If not, suggest that she try to resolve the situation directly. Following the correct chain of command, suggest that she first schedule a meeting with her teacher. You can offer to be present. Girls take pride in approaching their teachers and resolving issues; they also know they earn adults' respect when they are proactive. But if that doesn't help, a visit with her guidance counselor or adviser is probably in order. As a parent, it may relieve you to know firsthand that there are other support networks at school available to your daughter; this situation and its solution are not all on your shoulders.

Beyond getting through the school year more happily and successfully, girls who are able to develop and maintain strong connections learn lessons far more valuable than good grades. At some point, your daughter will have to get along with people she finds difficult, whether they are professors, bosses, roommates, or coworkers. Strong social skills will enable her to minimize unpleasantness, work out differences, combat stress, and benefit from relationships that are empowering.

CHAPTER 11

Taking the Next Step: Troubleshooting

At this point, the pressures holding your daughter back—the transitions, social insecurities, perfectionism, distracting problems, or feelings of being undervalued—are no longer so hidden. Now that you know more about what is specifically stressing her, you are probably thinking about what you can do differently. Should you give her space or time to mature? Find her a tutor? A therapist? Would a new school give her a fresh start in a more supportive environment? If you learned anything so far about teen girls, you know that offering help can be a tricky business.

While one daughter reacts defensively and indignantly when her parents try to encourage her or offer advice, another is grateful for the support. Throughout these pages you have also seen how many parents are so overly involved in their daughters' achievements that their well-meaning efforts backfire. So you might well be wondering when it *does* make sense to intervene. And if you do decide to step in, what is the right plan of action?

Many of you reading this book are already at your wit's end. As a teacher, you may be frustrated by trying to help a teenage girl perform as capably as you think she can. As a parent, you may believe that you have tried everything imaginable to motivate your daughter—and still nothing is working. In fact, it may seem that your life now revolves around reminding her of her responsibilities, enforcing rules so her homework gets done, and monitoring her grades. If so, the time you spend with your daughter is probably tense, unpleasant, and sometimes even painful. Not only is she resisting your help, but she also may be withdrawing or getting inexplicably angrier by the day.

This is what happened to the frustrated parents of a fifteen-year-old sophomore who recently consulted with me. As they described the situation, "We've taken away everything there is to take away—the cell phone, the Internet, the TV. We've forbidden Hannah's boyfriend to call the house or see her during the week. But her grades haven't improved at all. We just don't know what else to do." These parents were confused about their next step.

After I spoke with Hannah, I understood why all their solutions were falling flat. Although she, too, was upset and wanted to do better in school, she felt stuck. For her, the compelling problem was not grades, but rather her dreadful relationship with her parents. She dwelled on feeling wrongly blamed, misunderstood, and, deep down, terribly hurt:

> *We just don't get along, my parents and me. They're always on my back. They expect me to know where I want to go to college and what I want to be. My mom is always mad at something. She found out I got three C's last night and we had a minifight. They say they're not angry, just disappointed. They say they never ground me; they call it a lifestyle change, which is worse. I can't hang out with anyone till my grades get up, and I can't go online. She should be thankful I want to have people over here instead of going to parties with sketchy people and drugs.*

Regardless of whether your family life resembles Hannah's or is headed that way, the first order of business in helping your teenage daughter to be more successful is maintaining—or restoring—the calm and goodwill in your relationship with her. Here are troubleshooting tips and advice to consider, regardless of your daughter's situation at the moment.

Call a Time-out

If you aren't getting anywhere, part of the problem may be that emotions are too intense and conversations are overly heated. No one can think rationally when overwhelmed by feelings, especially an adolescent girl or a worried parent. Call a time-out on discussing "the problem" for a few days. During this cooling down period, stick to neutral topics and enjoy each other's company. Even issues that seem terribly urgent may look less so when everyone is more composed and in control.

Look at the Bright Side

Especially when nervous energy is peaking, it is easy for everyone to become mired in negativity. All you can focus on is what is wrong with your daughter—and how badly she is likely to turn out. Instead, deliberately note what she is doing well. Not only will you feel better, but also, when you catch her doing something right and praise her for it, she will too. Her confidence will soar—and her efforts along with it.

Put Things in Perspective

Under stress, it is hard to remember that your daughter is growing and maturing. Remind yourself about any rough patches in her past. What helped her through them back then? It may also help to talk to friends or relatives who have older children. Accomplished young adults were not always such successful students, athletes, or friends when they were teenagers. It is reassuring to learn that many struggled—some with serious problems—and yet turned out just fine.

Initiate a Fresh Discussion

No matter how wise your words, if they haven't worked before, don't repeat them—or hope to find new ones that are sure to turn your daughter around. Instead, talk with her just to get *her* take on the situation. What does she need? What would she like? If she says she hates school, find out more. Listen attentively and open-mindedly. When you know what it feels like to walk in your daughter's shoes, you will have a better sense of how to help. And if you can't alleviate problems, at least you can make them bearable by empathizing and supporting her. Giving her permission to speak about her genuine feelings is a gift to her sense of self.

Monitor Your Expectations

Whatever your daughter says about her difficulties, try to react nonjudgmentally. There may be nothing to do except listen or modify your expectations. Your daughter may not be interested in school or her favorite sport anymore, or she may be incapable of meeting certain goals right now. Remember that teens develop in fits and starts. Many girls don't especially like—or thrive—in high school. Some find their niche later on, in college or while working. Your daughter's problem may be temporary, but the wedge you drive into your relationship while trying to fix it could be permanent.

Wipe the Slate Clean

To prevent the parent-teen relationship from unraveling, you may have to start over with a clean slate. Rescinding all of your daughter's punishments can lift her mood and make her more amenable to your suggestions. To create a positive atmosphere, you might ask her to earn her privileges with responsible behavior. As one example, if she finishes her homework assignments one week, she gets a certain amount of time on the phone or computer the following week. As you have learned, it is best to engage your daughter in the negotiation process and to make the goals positive, specific, appropriate, and achievable.

Relieve Her Stress

- *Be her advocate.* Although you don't want to do this on a routine basis, when she is overwhelmed by many tests or assignments all at once or is too tired to stay up late studying, say, "Enough is enough." Write a note to her teacher excusing her lateness, demonstrating that her health and well-being come first.
- *Give her a mental health day.* Sometimes she just needs a break from school. Let her stay home and rest, catch up, or organize her closet. Though this might be hard for perfectionists, most girls enjoy the respite—and the support. This also gives your daughter the message that school is not the be-all and end-all.

+ *Lighten her schedule.* Ask your daughter to choose among her activities rather than trying to do everything. Initially she may resist, but when she knows what it feels like to be less stressed, she will probably be relieved and grateful.

+ *Let her change activities.* Your daughter may be in a rut because she is not doing what she really wants to do. If she is happier, she might become livelier, more enthusiastic, and inclined to make an effort in other, less appealing areas.

+ *Help her regain her balance.* Girls often need guidance to find the right balance in their lives. Imbalances—either all work and no play or all play and no work—inspire neither good coping skills nor success.

+ *Reduce distractions.* Many teens claim they can multitask— that is, talk on the phone and respond to instant messages, all while doing their work. But it is physically impossible to concentrate on this many different tasks at once. Suggest that your daughter make certain activities sacred and allot them her undivided attention.

+ *Rethink expectations for her activities.* If your daughter wants to quit playing the piano or swimming, clarify your expectations. Do you consider playing an instrument or exercising to be family norms, part of your values and lifestyle, or do you want her to become a superstar to bask in her reflected glory?

Have Her Evaluated

If you still have nagging questions about the cause of your daughter's struggles, I recommend having her evaluated. No matter what other people are telling you, if you sense there's a problem, trust your gut feelings. When I evaluate girls, I find that parents' suspicions are almost always right. Testing can tell you once and for all about your daughter's aptitude, her learning style, and whether there are gaps in her achievement that suggest a specific learning disorder. Also, a psychoeducational evaluation will assess her organizational skills, attention, and memory, and let you know whether anxiety, depression, or other emotional disorders are a factor in your daughter's struggles. Follow the guidelines I outlined in Chapter 4 on pages 101–3.

Find a Therapist

There are many reasons to consider therapy for your daughter: to deal with specific issues such as perfectionism, personal traumas, or social isolation; to help her learn more about herself; to develop better coping skills; or to improve how your family communicates, gets along, and handles pressures for achievement. Even when you don't fully understand why, if your daughter says she wants to see someone, it is especially important to follow through. Consult a mental health center or clinic in your community. You can also ask a trusted friend, physician, teacher, guidance counselor, or state professional association for a referral to a licensed, experienced clinician.

Transfer Her to a Different School

As a last resort, you may wonder if transferring your daughter to a different school is the answer, especially if she feels insecure or undervalued where she is now. This decision can be agonizing. Anxiety surrounding achievement spurs parents to find the ideal school—the one environment that would guarantee their daughter's success.

School is only one part of the equation for success, but teens must believe their schools offer meaningful work and a fair chance of succeeding. The essential questions to consider are these: Does your daughter's school enable her to feel generally competent and good about herself? Does the school community value her particular talents and interests? How does the school environment affect her level of stress? Consider how well these school characteristics match your daughter's needs:

Academic Selectivity. Much of the nervous energy about achievement these days comes from pressure on parents to send their children to academically selective high schools that will maximize their chances of being accepted at elite colleges. Surrounded by classmates who excel and are held to higher standards for excellence, some girls do rise to the challenge. Yet new research on school selectivity and self-concept—how a girl thinks and feels about herself—should give you pause.

Studying four thousand fifteen-year-olds from twenty-six countries, psychologists Herbert W. March, of the University of Western Sydney, and Kit-Tai Hau, of the Chinese University of Hong Kong, found that students in academically selective schools generally have a lower self-concept than those in nonselective schools. A girl's self-concept is based on her own academic achievement level and also on comparing her accomplishments to those of her classmates.

Calling this phenomenon the big-fish-little-pond effect, researchers found that students suffer when they are average or below average in comparison to their classmates in academically selective schools. Seeing themselves as small fish in a pond with larger fish (brighter students), their self-concept deteriorates, adversely affecting their educational choices and decisions, effort and persistence, and subsequent success. For example, if they have to work extremely hard to get average grades, many students eventually come to think that it is not worth their effort.

In contrast, when girls transfer to less selective schools (smaller ponds), they become bigger fish (among the lower achieving students). This boosts their academic self-concept and their performance. This makes sense. Girls consistently tell me that they have the worst time in school and feel most like failures when "other students are much smarter than I am," "I do terrible on a test everyone did well on," and "I realized it didn't matter how much I worked; the geniuses would always have better grades."

Until researchers identify why certain students benefit from being small fish in large ponds, you should think long and hard before placing—let alone *pushing*—your daughter to attend an academically selective school, or enrolling her in accelerated and honors classes against her school's recommendations.

Degree of Structure. A teen's personality and learning style often determine whether she thrives at a particular school. If your daughter is constitutionally rule governed, she may feel more secure in a highly structured school that offers clear expectations, schedules, guidelines, and limits. But if she wants to make her own decisions and needs more autonomy, she might feel claustrophobic or constrained. In that case, a school with fewer rules and higher tolerance for student choice would be a better match.

In rare cases, I believe some girls do best in boarding schools. These teens need the structure often provided by mandated daily study periods and benefit from working closely with teachers whom they get to know in other capacities around the school. In addition, some girls can concentrate on their own work better when they are away from intense ongoing family struggles or untenable situations at home.

Learning Opportunities. If your daughter enjoys reading, writing, and memorizing, a traditional school may suit her style. However, if she is more creative, right-brained, or energetic, she might flourish when desk work is deemphasized—for example, when teachers assign hands-on projects, experiments, and labs. If your daughter dislikes tests and papers, she might like the chance to demonstrate knowledge verbally (through oral reports) or creatively (through drawings, dioramas, or PowerPoint presentations). Another consideration is whether she prefers to work alone or enjoys collaborating; schools vary widely in their emphasis on individual versus group projects. Also, if she is passionate about certain topics, a school that offers independent studies may be a good fit.

Teaching Philosophies. Especially if your middle school daughter is struggling, you might think about her teachers' styles. Jacquelynne S. Eccles, a professor at the University of Michigan, discounts the common notion that seventh graders typically lose motivation because of teen hormones, their increased social interest, and their detachment from adults. Instead, she points to ineffective teachers: those who are less confident, don't challenge kids, use more controlling disciplinary tactics, and develop lower-quality emotional relationships with their students. Other researchers report that ineffective teachers seem annoyed by questions and mistakes, which was also reported frequently by girls responding to my own survey.

In contrast, effective teachers emphasize that being unsure, asking questions, and learning from mistakes are natural parts of learning. They interrupt their lessons to ask if students remember previous concepts and to clarify current concepts. Thus they ensure that everyone arrives at the right answers. Also, successful teachers use humor and other motivational supports to make students feel comfortable asking for help.

Coed Versus Same-Sex Schools. If you have ever wondered if your daughter would be better off at an all-girl or coed school, you should know that the jury is still out. Although the 1992 American Association of University Women report advocated separate math and science classes for girls, later research declared the data inconclusive. Results were highly individual; some girls in some settings benefited more than others. It was also unclear to what degree the observed differences were attributable to the smaller, more nurturing classes offered by independent schools.

In a new trend, a few private schools are beginning to separate boys and girls during the trying and tumultuous middle school years. This practice is based on the understanding that males and females have different rates of physical, emotional, and cognitive maturation during this time period. As girls describe so vividly within these pages, their learning styles are also vastly different. Whereas boys are active, outspoken, competitive, and intent upon getting the work done, girls are more interested in doing their work correctly, getting along well with their classmates, and pleasing their teachers.

An interesting new study of test performance supports this educational model. Psychologists found that college women performed markedly better when they took math tests in the company of all females rather than with all males.

Schools that segregate boys and girls during the middle school years have pros and cons. If your daughter is in a great rush to grow up, a respite from the pressures and temptations of boy-girl interactions during the school day may be advantageous. Or if your daughter tends to be unusually intimidated by boys, attending all-girl classes might enable her to hold on to her voice. On the other hand, she might benefit from the chance to interact with boys and stand up for herself in the classroom. This is yet another factor to add to the mix.

Individual Strengths Valued. Especially when your daughter is not doing well and feels like a square peg, it makes sense to consider whether her talents would be more valued by another school. According to Robert J. Sternberg, past president of the American Psychological Association, our educational system currently taps two important skills: memory and analysis. He has said that "students who are adept at these two skills tend to profit from the educational system because the ability, instruction, and achievement tests we use all largely measure products and processes emanating from these two kinds of skills." Children whose strengths lie elsewhere tend to be shortchanged.

Dr. Sternberg argues, for example, that when kids do poorly on ability and achievement tests, their teachers treat them as losers and create harmful self-fulfilling prophecies. To enable all students to succeed, even those who are not strong in memory or analysis, he and his colleagues encourage adding creative and practical learning to curricula. Specifically, they recommend addressing "the other three R's" in education—reasoning, resilience, and responsibility.

Apart from her studies, your daughter will do better when her teachers recognize and build upon her strengths. For example, girls enthuse about classes in which their teachers ask them to read their work aloud to the class, tutor other students, or publish their writing in the school newspaper or literary magazine. Do your daughter's teachers take the time to get to know her? Do they notice her leadership potential or artistic flair? Do they suggest that she run for office or help out with the scenery in the school play?

Degree of Pressure. Is your daughter's school making her feel more or less stressed out? Even the most resilient girls are crushed by excessive pressure. One highly achieving teen describes an over-the-top workload: "I haven't even taken my tenth grade world history final yet, and already I got this seven-page packet of assignments in the mail that I have to do over the summer for my AP U.S. history course next year. At no time do they ever let me feel like I'm done, like I can just relax."

Your daughter might be better off in a school that is low-key or takes pains to avoid distressing her—especially if she is anxious, perfectionistic, or just needs time to draw, audition for plays, train for a marathon, or write in her journal. Some schools make this possible by decreasing the number and complexity of assignments to reduce stress and make students' workloads more reasonable.

Responding to parents' feedback and concerns, for example, one independent high school I visited now asks teachers to pay closer attention to whether homework is significant for learning. They are sensitive to the value of teens spending time with their families and eating dinner together. Another school took out the cuts in middle school athletics because "it made a huge difference in whether our girls were stressed out." Check out whether schools are aware of this issue and how they are handling it.

Assessment of Progress. It is important for your daughter to believe that evaluations of her progress are fair and valid, and that her teachers have a good handle on both her strengths and her weaknesses. Does her school emphasize grades or other measures of achievement? Is she best served by numerical grades, narrative reports, a combination of both, or a pass/fail option? Like many girls, the chance for self-assessment might appeal to her. One study found that girls but not boys improve when given rubrics that contain explicit criteria for good and poor writing. Girls benefit because knowing what counts in good writing takes the subjectivity out of grading. They are less apt to feel their performance is based on whether or not the teacher likes them. If the assessment process works well, your daughter believes her report cards provide valid and helpful feedback about her work.

The Case Against Switching. Before you decide to transfer your daughter to a new school, though, consider these caveats:

1. Few schools are perfect—and no school is perfect for everyone. No matter how wonderful the teachers, creative the curriculum, or fabulous the facilities, it is not right for every teenage girl. You can't assume your daughter will definitely do better there.

2. Girls do not require an exceptional academic setting in order to excel, or even to do well—even if they are extremely bright or gifted.

3. Your daughter's school does not have to meet all of her needs. Enrichment classes, recreational activities, and skill-building programs can also nourish her.

4. Experts argue that learning to cope with less than ideal school situations—for example, understimulating classes, irritating teachers, "unfair" rules and grading policies—is more educational, in the long run, than anything covered in the curriculum.

5. Your daughter may resist changing schools even if she is unhappy because the unknown is scary. As described in Chapter 4, transitions are usually challenging.

6. Transferring schools is not always the answer. Teens who shuffle from one school to another usually discover that it is not their schools that are making them unhappy; when their problems follow them wherever they go, they feel like repeat failures.

TRIUMPHING OVER STRESS

Regardless of where your daughter attends school, you will help her make the best of her situation. Besides, you have the perspective now that even girls who are well matched with their schools don't always sail through their teen years. When she struggles, your daughter needs to rely on her parents and teachers. With support, she can cope better with stress, know herself well, take charge of her own efforts, and figure out what she needs to improve. Self-knowledge, confidence, a balanced life, and a positive outlook effectively remove the barriers to your daughter's success. I believe that Miriam, a *Girls' Life* reader, best exemplifies this resilient attitude:

> *School is what you make of it. It can be a great place to expand your mind, develop skills you'll need later in life, hang with your friends, and get amazing insights from teachers who have lived life and know amazing things to tell you. Or, if you make it so, it can be a big stressful experience that you dread and loathe 24/7. Some of my friends are very uptight about grades—I see how they get stressed out over a 93 on a test and that's why I am convinced that I can't be. I worry about college every once in a while, but you just have to always remember that you can do only the best you can do, and it's never, ever worth it to push yourself over the limit. I still think learning can be fun, but it all depends on your attitude.*

Despite your resolve and your daughter's best efforts, it is wise to anticipate that neither she nor you can be completely immune to stress. In this era of intense pressure about achievement, it is hard to imagine that possibility. At times your daughter will become anxious—and so will you.

My high school focus group became nearly electrified with nervous energy one mid-December morning when Meghan, a junior, reported that a senior friend who had applied to Cornell on an early decision basis had been rejected. Sensing the mood in the room, Valerie quickly tried to reassure the other girls. "You know, my older sister is looking at a college right now that looks at how much community service you did," she said. "They want to see that you're a well-rounded person. She gets good grades. She doesn't do well on standardized tests, but they didn't care."

"Oh, that's just like me!" exclaimed another junior, clearly relieved.

"Wow!" said a third, slowly shaking her head reverently. "There's hope." With that, the anxiety in the room disappeared.

Relieved from the pressure to raise a supergirl, you, too, can be hopeful. You can relax and trust in the maturational process through which your daughter will learn and grow. You'll feel more confident of using your instincts to know when to guide her, when to intervene, and when to let her work things out on her own. With this freedom, you will enable her to stay connected to her inner life. Best of all, you'll be able to sit back and watch with wonder while your daughter evolves into the interesting and accomplished young woman she is destined to become.

Index